# Robin Belfield

Robin Belfield is a theatre director and writer. After graduating from the University of Bristol, he was awarded a place on the Regional Theatre Young Directors Scheme and since then has been making work with many of the major UK theatre companies including the Royal Shakespeare Company, the National Theatre (where he has also taught verbatim-theatre techniques), Nuffield Southampton Theatres, Bristol Old Vic, Watermill Theatre, Dukes (Lancaster) and Theatre Royal Bath. Robin has also worked extensively in a number of UK drama schools including the Royal Welsh College of Music and Drama and the Oxford School of Drama. He is one half of Belfield and Slater Musicals.

# MAKING THEATRE

The **Making Theatre** series of practical handbooks introduces theatre-makers, directors, students and audiences to the key concepts, principles and techniques for making popular styles of contemporary theatre. Each book is written by a working practitioner, drawing on their own experience in the field.

**CREATING WORLDS**
*How to Make Immersive Theatre*
Jason Warren

**TELLING THE TRUTH**
*How to Make Verbatim Theatre*
Robin Belfield

*The publisher welcomes suggestions for further titles in the series.*

# Robin Belfield

# Telling the Truth

## How to Make Verbatim Theatre

NICK HERN BOOKS
London
www.nickhernbooks.co.uk

A Nick Hern Book

*Telling the Truth: How to Make Verbatim Theatre*
first published in Great Britain in 2018
as a paperback original by Nick Hern Books Limited,
The Glasshouse, 49a Goldhawk Road, London W12 8QP

Cover image: *London Road* by Alecky Blythe and Adam Cork
(National Theatre, London, 2011); photograph © Tristram Kenton

Designed and typeset by Nick Hern Books, London
Printed and bound in Great Britain by
Ashford Colour Press, Gosport, Hampshire

A CIP catalogue record for this book
is available from the British Library

ISBN 978 1 84842 491 3

MIX
Paper from
responsible sources
FSC
www.fsc.org
FSC® C011748

*This book is dedicated to
Rebecca, Cora and Elijah Belfield,
as am I*

# Contents

# Introduction

## What is Verbatim Theatre?

It's a bit like asking, 'what is theatre?' Theatre can be so many different things, encompassing so many different genres and styles. It can also be created in a multitude of different ways, a vast spectrum of techniques and processes that suit the practitioner and the work. It's hard to define verbatim as a genre or a type; some people refer to it as 'documentary theatre', which in many circumstances it is, but that does slightly reduce its potential. Instead, if we must categorise it, it would seem to fit more comfortably under the banner of 'techniques and processes'.

Verbatim theatre refers to the way a piece is created and, more specifically, the materials used to create it. **Verbatim theatre is a play constructed with words that were *actually* spoken by *real* people**, rather than created via the imagination of a playwright or devised by theatre-makers. It is this double layer (actual words and real people) that gives verbatim theatre its authority, perhaps more so than other imagined plays, because it can claim to present reality in a way that the imagination cannot. An imagined play, exploring real events or real people, however well researched, still relies on some semblance of dramatic licence. This of course can still present a truth, but it is seen through the filter of the playwright's imagination. With verbatim plays the opposite is true; there the practitioner still acts as a filter, but is guided by the authenticity of the **actual words spoken in the original context**.

## About This Book

There are several books available that explore the concept of verbatim theatre, its history, its values and its limitations as a theatrical form. But that is not the aim of this book. This is, as the title suggests, a handbook and a practical guide through the processes of making theatre using verbatim material.

Having seen many verbatim plays previously, and having created my own, in 2009 I was given the opportunity to assist director Angus Jackson as he worked on *The Power of Yes* – a new verbatim play by David Hare exploring the financial crisis that had hit the world's banks the year before. Watching both Angus and David go through a process of collecting, editing, shaping and eventually presenting the information and opinions given by those 'in-the-know' was a fascinating and inspiring experience. Following this I became more and more interested in the process of making verbatim theatre, and increasingly aware that (as with all theatre) there are as many different practices as there are practitioners. I am grateful to the National Theatre Studio, Sussex Actors Studio and also the Danish National School of Playwriting, who all invited me to lead various short courses for drama teachers and emerging theatre-makers, these opportunities allowed me to consolidate my own approach to this work.

This handbook is that process explained and explored, step by step. It is also an opportunity to compare the processes of other practitioners (actors, writers and so on), taking a closer look at specific examples of their work and how they went about making it. As you will see there is no one single approach, but a spectrum, depending on how dogmatically you apply the rules or whether you choose to bend them a little.

The process of using verbatim material to create a piece of theatre will require you to ask lots of questions in order to make the right decisions ('right' for you and the particular piece), and also to ask questions about the decisions you've made. Through my conversations with leading practitioners and developing my own practice I have found that to make verbatim theatre you will need the following four qualities:

• Rigour

• Accuracy

• Clarity

• Patience

As a verbatim theatre-maker you are (or will soon become) part playwright, part director, part practitioner and facilitator, part journalist, part detective – and in all that, these four qualities emerge time and time again, at every stage of the process and throughout this book. If you are not prepared to apply them all, I suggest you read no further!

## How to Use This Book

Each of the following chapters takes a closer look at each of the steps in the process of making verbatim theatre and will serve as an introduction for those embarking on this journey for the very first time, but also as a reference guide for those returning to verbatim. Included along the way are **case studies** that put different examples of verbatim plays under the spotlight; **interviews** with different practitioners on their approaches; **hints and tips**; and **activities and practical exercises** to help you deepen or investigate your own practice.

It may be worth noting from the outset that most of the activities laid out in this book are based on the assumption that you aren't working alone, but that you have other company members (actors, students or collaborators) who will be working with you to create this piece. Working with an ensemble will give you an array of perspectives and critical thinking which will be of real value throughout the process. However, if you are working alone, these activities will still be a useful guide to assist you in the early stages before you assemble a company together to perform your work.

So whatever your previous experience and your current circumstances, I hope this book will prove a useful guide to assist you as you navigate through the various challenges you might face at each stage of the process, enabling you to consolidate these methods into techniques and practices of your own.

# 1. The Subject

## How to choose a subject

Verbatim theatre isn't restricted to one particular category or genre of performance. The techniques used when creating verbatim theatre can apply to any genre; but the decision about what style and form your piece will take must begin and end with the subject you want to explore.

One of the first questions any playwright must ask as they embark on creating a play is: 'what is the story I need to tell?' The same is true of the verbatim practitioner, although I would argue that finding the 'story' is part of the process, rather than the catalyst for the process. Your catalyst is the **subject**. The subject is what you set out to explore; it may be to investigate a broad theme, or indeed take a microscope to something much more specific. Either way, this process is about asking questions and being open to the answers, rather than approaching it with a preformed 'story'. If you know the answers, write a play. Plenty of plays are based on real events, written to present a particular angle or point of view. But verbatim is different. The material you will need has not been collected or collated yet, some of it won't even exist yet, so it is impossible to come to any definitive conclusions until you have asked your questions and begun your investigations. You may of course have an idea of what the

1

'story' will be; all I'm suggesting, and will continue to remind you, is that you need to remain open to surprise.

So the first question for us is: **what is the subject of your story?** Once we know the answer to this, we can then begin to move through the process. You may not have a clue, in which case this chapter will enable you to explore different options and take you through a process of selection. It may be that you have a small inkling, a germ of an idea perhaps, or indeed may already have a pretty clear answer to the question. In these cases this chapter becomes a sort of health check for your thinking. And that's something we are going to have to get used to – checking and rechecking our decision-making.

## Subject Categories

In the broadest possible terms, I would say that most verbatim plays fall into two categories – those based on **events** and those based on a particular **theme**.

### Events

It is not surprising that many of the most famous verbatim plays are inspired by a singular event, or series of events. Be it a natural disaster or a more personal event, the verbatim play allows an audience to hear the testimony of those eyewitnesses – the people who were there, who saw it happen and felt (or feel) its consequences. Often an event might warrant further exploration, investigation or perhaps just simply the recognition that there is a story that needs to be told.

It would be safe to say that most event-based verbatim plays are in fact responding to a current event, rather than an historical one. The immediacy of verbatim theatre makes it an ideal forum to explore an event that is current and relevant to its audience. It may be that you are spurred on by an event that has happened in the last few days; it might also be true that although the event is in the past (perhaps still within living memory), the consequences are still keenly felt.

### *The Colour of Justice* by Richard Norton-Taylor
### Tricycle Theatre, London (1999)

Stephen Lawrence was a young black man who, in 1993, was murdered in a racially motivated attack while he waited for a bus in London. This high-profile case was prominent in the news for a several years after, as the authorities failed to secure a conviction. In 1998 a public inquiry was held, led by retired High Court judge Sir William Macpherson, and in 1999 his report accused the Metropolitan Police of institutional racism.

That same year Nicolas Kent, then Artistic Director of the Tricycle Theatre in London, produced *The Colour of Justice*. This verbatim play was based on the transcripts from the Stephen Lawrence Inquiry. In an article published in the *Guardian*, Norton-Taylor described the power of the piece:

> We could expose the racism – institutional, the judge
> called it, and of the Metropolitan Police – in a single piece
> for the theatre, something more powerful, and with a much
> greater impact, than any number of shorter, inevitably
> intermittent, articles in newspapers, or short clips on the
> radio or television news.[1]

Following its run at the Tricycle, *The Colour of Justice* transferred to the West End and was also turned into a television drama. Interestingly, the 'event' on which the play is based is the Inquiry led by Macpherson – the murder itself happened some years earlier. The subject is of course the brutal murder of Stephen Lawrence, but the story is something quite different. The story aimed to shed light on the investigation and the conduct of the Metropolitan Police in the wake of a huge public outcry at the failure and apparent racism of the police force. The subject remained extremely topical and raised wider questions about modern society, making it both important and urgent.

1. 'Verbatim plays pack more punch than the papers' by Richard Norton-Taylor, *Guardian*, 22 October 2014.

## Activity: The Search

○ *News sources*   We have to start somewhere, so why not with the news? What are the stories that are perhaps dominating the media, or perhaps those that are hidden away in the middle pages? In small groups or individually, take one of the following news sources:

- Local newspaper
- National newspaper (broadsheet)
- National newspaper (tabloid)
- Television news (BBC, ITV, Channel 4, Sky, etc.)
- Internet news site (Buzzfeed, Associated Press, etc.)

○ *Speed-read*   Set a time limit to go through the source, relatively quickly, and highlight or bookmark all the stories that spark your attention.

○ *Review*   Read back over your selection of stories and choose just one to investigate further. *Keep the other stories to hand; you are allowed to change your mind, or indeed may want to revisit them another time.*

○ *Read in detail*   Now focus on the one story you have selected. Read and re-read, making notes of any key information.

○ *Share your findings*   Have two or more people/groups chosen the same story? Is there a link between them? If so, discuss why you might have been drawn to the same or similar stories? Discoveries will be made in the debate, whether it's with collaborators, students or critical friends, so share your ideas and test your thinking.

○ *Ask 'why verbatim?'*   Finally, ask each group to summarise in a few points why their chosen story needs to be told using verbatim theatre, instead of using any other theatrical form.

*HINT: This, like other activities in this handbook, is best undertaken with strict time limits. If you are working with a group of actors or students, being able to process information quickly and accurately will be an extremely useful skill to develop as you continue this process of making verbatim theatre.*

## Historical Events

You may prefer to investigate an historical event. A huge number of plays take on historical subjects, and an audience permits the playwright a certain amount of licence to invent the missing pieces – the dialogue behind closed doors or the moments before and after a significant moment in history. But even though an audience gives this licence, they remain knowledgeable of the fact that it is in part a work of fiction and are satisfied to accept that in the cases where we just never know 'what really happened' at that particular time and place. So, offered the opportunity of real verbatim material and eyewitness testimony that opens a window into the past, an audience is able to get closer to 'what really happened' and, perhaps more importantly, *what it was really like to be there.*

The range of historical subjects is so vast it could be quite daunting just thinking about where to start! The activities below (pages 13–14) will facilitate a thorough questioning of whether your suggested subject is **relevant** or **important** – or ideally both! It is essential to ask yourself, why is it of interest or necessary to explore something historical? It could be a personal interest in the life of a particular person, or a major historical event. Equally it may have a wider relevance – a local or even national interest. Next you should answer the question: why verbatim theatre? Why not just write a play? Do you have the amount of material needed to create a piece of theatre, and what do you gain in presenting this material verbatim, rather than using it as research to feed your imagination?

On the face of it these questions may seem pedantic, but the point I'm trying to emphasise is that verbatim theatre is a technique with both huge possibilities and huge limitations. The foundation of every verbatim play is quality material; with historical events the search may be harder, but the rewards greater – to be able to expose real words, real thoughts, real experiences and prove the point: 'you couldn't make this stuff up!'

### *Up the Feeder, Down the 'Mouth* by ACH Smith
*Bristol Old Vic (1997 & 2001)*

Originally commissioned by Bristol Old Vic's then-Artistic Director Andy Hay, ACH Smith was asked to write a play in a 'documentary vein' about the Bristol Docks. Once one of the country's major ports, the docks in Bristol finally closed in the 1970s. The closure of the city's dockyards also signalled the end of a significant aspect of the city's history, as well as one of its major employers. Although clearly a historical piece, the culture of the docks – the stories, songs and so on – still remain in the city's living memory, with most native Bristolians able to make a direct connection to life and work on the docks.

Such was the strength of feeling towards the docks and the lives of those who worked there, the play was a resounding success. It was revived in 2001, this time in a site-specific production on the dockside. It's worth referencing this play as one of the strongest examples of verbatim theatre that has a huge relevance to a particular community. Despite it being 'historical', the play could hardly be considered high up on our Important/Urgent Axis (see pages 13–14), but it was and remains to this day hugely relevant to the local populace. The subject was the Bristolians, and the play was for Bristolians – so much so that both productions included a number of local amateur performers as a 'community chorus', many of whom had direct experience of the dockers' way of life.

ACH Smith interviewed some fifty dockers (and their families) to capture both their personal stories and the wider sociopolitical context, in order to illustrate the ultimate demise of the Bristol Docks.

In 2014, ACH Smith was invited to write a similar play about the Clifton Suspension Bridge, another icon of the Bristol; we will explore his second historical verbatim play later on in this book.

Whether you decide to take on a current or historical event as the subject for your verbatim piece, both have their advantages and disadvantages. While a modern event is current and information about it is readily available, you will also need to be aware, especially if it is a tragic event, that your play may be touching on issues that are still extremely sensitive. We will discuss the ethical issues of verbatim theatre in Chapter Six, however, it's worth noting early if the topic is likely to cause upset or offence. On the other hand, with historical events, although the emotional connection may not be as fresh, you may still face challenges – the further back you go, the more likely your source material is to become scarce. Remember, verbatim theatre is 'in their own words', so if your subject (or eyewitnesses) are no longer living, you may find it harder to gain access to those words – letters, diaries, speeches, interviews and so on. It may also be the case that information gathered is far less reliable and this may mean you are required to do much more research in order to corroborate your initial findings or source material.

With both current and historical events, you have the freedom to discover which aspects of the event interest you and those that you think will be of interest to your audience. Do you take a broad view and try to report on the event as a whole – the causes as well as the consequences? Alternatively, do you prefer to take a microscopic view on a smaller aspect – shining the spotlight on something that has previously been overlooked, or making a seemingly minor character into the central protagonist?

*Other event-based verbatim plays include:*

- *Katrina* **by Jonathan Holmes** (Jericho House in association with Young Vic, 2009) – Described as a 'testimony play' it was staged four years after the devastating Hurricane Katrina hit New Orleans.

- *The Laramie Project* **by Moisés Kaufman** (Tectonic Theater, 2000) – Charted the reactions of local residents following the homophobic murder of student Matthew

Shepard in Laramie, Wyoming, USA. In a second play, the same theatre company returned to Laramie ten years later, interviewing the same people they had encountered in the initial play, and documenting how their reactions – and lives – had changed.

- *The Tribunal Plays* (Tricycle Theatre) – During Nicolas Kent's tenure as Artistic Director of the Tricycle, he produced many plays, like *The Colour of Justice*, which were based on the records and transcripts of high-profile tribunals. Others include *Bloody Sunday: Scenes from the Saville Inquiry* (2005) and *Justifying War: Scenes from the Hutton Inquiry* (2003).

- *The Riots* by **Gillian Slovo** (Tricycle Theatre, 2011) – Investigating the events and responses to riots in London, which were a reaction to the death of Mark Duggan by the police.

- *Little Revolution* by **Alecky Blythe** (Almeida Theatre, 2014) – This was Alecky Blythe's response to the same London riots, although her play was produced some three years after the event.

## Themes

By taking a theme or broader issue as the subject, your verbatim theatre play will give you the opportunity to link together different events, responses and opinions. You may even be interested in spanning a much wider time frame, combining both historical and modern source material.

## Home by Nadia Fall
## National Theatre, London (2013)

*Home*'s creator Nadia Fall recorded interviews with residents and workers in a hostel in East London. It questioned and explored the issue of homelessness amongst young people and was performed in the NT's temporary venue, The Shed. Although homelessness has arguably been an issue in the UK for centuries, the issue of homelessness and young people seemed very pertinent at the time of the play's opening. A steep rise in homelessness in London, combined with changes to the government's housing policy, certainly added to the topicality of the play.

Following its initial run, it was revived the following year; substantial changes had to be made to the script in order to maintain the play's relevance, and the creative team returned to re-interview many of the original characters. In an article for the BBC, Fall suggested that 'about eighty-five per cent of what is heard is pure verbatim. There's artistic licence in the music and staging – it is a creative process – but my own responsibility is to what I see as the truth of the situation.'[2] The production was celebrated not just for its eye-opening testimony but also for the use of live music, beat-boxing and humour.

Similar to ACH Smith's play *Up the Feeder, Down the 'Mouth*, this is a play very specific to its location and therefore has a specific relevance to a London audience. However, in this example it's hard to imagine that the play would have had any less impact if it had been produced in Birmingham, Edinburgh or indeed any of the UK's major cities.

THE SUBJECT

2. 'Home at National Theatre shines a light on homelessness' by Kev Geoghegan, BBC News online, 27 August 2013.

To kickstart your thinking as to what issue or topic you might like to tackle with your verbatim piece, below are a few themes and sub-categories that may act as a prompt.

*Health*

- Physical health issues
- Mental health
- Body image
- Alcohol/drugs

*Social*

- Bullying
- Anti-social behaviour
- Human behaviour or habits (e.g. personal/sexual relationships, religious/cult practices, gang culture, gambling, protests/riots)
- Modern life (e.g. social media, youth, ageing)

*Political*

- Local council decisions (e.g. new developments, closure of local amenities)
- Schools and education
- The armed forces and war
- Legal issues (e.g. crimes, major court cases, tribunals/inquiries)
- Housing
- Transport
- Poverty and wealth

*Environmental*

- Climate change
- Animal welfare
- Air quality
- Food production and standards
- Water pollution
- Energy production (e.g. nuclear, renewable, fracking, fossil fuels)
- Waste management

## Activity: Choosing a 'Theme'

○ *Take on a sub-category*   In small groups, take one sub-category each and discuss the suggested themes and issues, which would make interesting and/or provocative verbatim plays? Are there any not listed that are also worth consideration?

○ *List the titles*   Draw up a list of possible titles for each idea to share with the group.

○ *Share your ideas and titles*   Are there connections or links between the categories? Do these initial thoughts spark new ideas?

*HINT: The best titles are pithy and above all clear, indicating to the audience (or in this case the other members of your group, class or company) what the chosen issue is.*

## The Challenge of Breadth

One of the key questions you will need to ask yourself when tackling a broad subject is: 'what will be the focus?' What lies at the heart of your piece? Is it a particular fact, statistic or phenomenon that you are trying to explore?

The breadth of your chosen theme may create challenges for you. Of course you want to choose a subject on which lots of interesting source material can be found; but you must remember your main objective in all this – to tell a story as clearly as possible. Using *Home* as an example, the issue of homelessness is huge, arguably too big for one play, so choices will have been made along the way as to the 'focus', or what we will go on to know as the particular 'story' the play is trying to tell. Nadia Fall chose to look at homelessness with respect to young people, which immediately focused the lens. But why not older people? Or women?

*Home* was clearly set in London; as I have already suggested, the subject would have remained topical whatever the location, but it would have been an entirely different play if the interviews were taken from the shelter in Cardiff, Belfast or Manchester – the dialect, the locations, the references, the turns of phrase – all those qualities that make verbatim testimony and ultimately the verbatim play unique. All of these alternatives are equally valid and interesting choices, and would have made equally strong productions; they were, nevertheless, choices that had to be made.

## Why You? Why Now?

Whether provoked by a specific event or a wider theme, the beauty of verbatim theatre is its capacity to capture and document a subject with more clarity and precision than a play invented by a playwright. As a consequence verbatim theatre often needs to be produced quickly, while that subject is still current or topical. Perhaps this is simply because verbatim theatre brilliantly offers the opportunity for investigation and interrogation of subjects that have a sense of social importance. That said, the obvious disadvantage of this is that verbatim plays can soon become out of date and irrelevant, as most seem to live and die with the public consciousness surrounding the subject.

Hopefully by now you have an idea of the subject that will form the starting point for your piece. If so, the next questions that are worth asking yourself are as follows:

- *Why is this an important subject for you to tackle?* Perhaps it has personal relevance, or is a contentious topic where you live? Perhaps you feel that it's a topic that warrants further investigation?

- *Why is it important you explore this subject now?* Perhaps it follows current (or recent) events? Perhaps it explores an aspect of our lives that seems particularly relevant? Perhaps it is to coincide with an anniversary of an historical event?

However, if you haven't yet settled on your subject, or if you are still wrestling with lots of ideas, here's a simple activity to assist your decision-making.

## Activity: The Important/Urgent Axis

○ *List all of your ideas*  If you are working with a class or group, you may want to divide them into smaller groups and give one or two ideas to each group. Each group will need one sheet of A4 paper per idea.

○ *Write a one-line synopsis*  How would you summarise each subject or story, in just one sentence? Write this synopsis along the bottom of the paper.

○ *Invent a title*  If you haven't already, give each idea a title and write it in large letters on the paper so it can be read from a distance.

○ *The Important/Urgent Axis*  Clear a space on the floor, or alternatively use a whiteboard or wall if you prefer. Mark out the two axes (see diagram below) by either laying down some rope, ribbon or string, or simply drawing them out.

○ *Make your judgements*  Each group should then place their ideas on the floor (or wall) making a judgement about how they correlate to the two axes. As they do, encourage them to explain their thinking to the rest of the group. Once all ideas have been laid out, you can facilitate a discussion to find out whether everyone agrees with all the placements or whether some need to be repositioned.

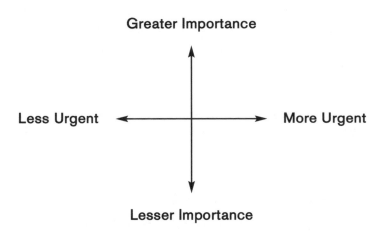

One might argue that the ideas placed in the uppermost right-hand quarter are the ones to pursue, those which are acknowledged as being the most 'important' and most 'urgent'. However, the labels of the axes are already dictating the tone of the piece and this may not be appropriate for you. If so, experiment with different labels such as 'Entertaining' or 'Relevant' and interchange them so as to test and debate your ideas. As we've already discussed, the discoveries will be made in the debate.

THE SUBJECT

It's important to recognise that right from the off you are applying value judgements to these subjects. These decisions are already starting to represent your opinion, your voice. As you'll see, your voice will be extremely valuable through this process, but it's worth making sure you are aware of the choices you are making and that they have a direct influence over what will become your verbatim play – what you choose to share with the audience and how. These choices are made throughout the process, but become especially important during the editing stage, which we will discuss in more detail in Chapter Five.

## Your Audience

Yes, those people that you expect, or hope, will come and see your verbatim play. It's all too easy to forget about (or ignore) them. In fact they should be central to your decision-making at every stage, so start off on the right foot and take them into consideration from the beginning.

Perhaps you have an audience ready and waiting – friends and family, the local community, or those who have previously attended or who follow your work. In which case the questions to ask are about relevance:

- *Are the subjects you have identified as relevant to the audience as they are to you?* Are they subjects that affect (or have affected) their lives directly?

Or:

- *Are these subjects relevant, but at present your audience is unaware of them?* Is there an opportunity for you to bring a specific topic into the public consciousness? Is your audience unaware of this subject through lack of information or denial?

Alternatively, your chosen subject may suggest a certain target audience; or perhaps you may have a specific remit or brief to fulfil which also dictates a certain audience demographic – young people, older people, a specific community or group. In cases like these, it's useful to road-test your thinking against these questions and activities in order to clarify your choices.

Being aware of who your intended audience is from the outset (and regularly reminding yourself) will help keep your decision-making in check and assist you in producing a verbatim play that is clear in its storytelling and balanced in its sharing of information.

# 2. The Research

*How to prepare and conduct interviews and get the most out of the research phase*

## Where to Start Your Research?

This next stage of the process might be best described as 'initial research', as once you have settled on the subject your job now is to amass as much information as you possibly can on that particular subject – the challenge now is to become an expert in your chosen field.

The collecting of information may continue right through until the performance, but obviously you will need to make early decisions for practical reasons – no actor is going to appreciate an massive addition of new or altered lines at the last minute! However, if your verbatim piece is at the top end of our Important/Urgent Axis (if you are looking at a very recent event for instance; pages 13–14), you may find that new information on the subject is being revealed daily and your material will need to reflect that information if you want the piece to be as current and relevant as possible.

A good example of this was David Hare's play *The Power of Yes* for the National Theatre. Whilst the production was in rehearsals, the world outside was still reeling in the aftermath of the financial crash of 2008, and although most of the material gathered was about the causes and immediate consequences of the event itself, the play still had to speak to an audience whose knowledge and opinions were shifting on an almost daily basis.

It may be a cliché to say, but it's certainly true that we really do live in a digital age and information on almost any subject is readily available to us at the click of a button. The nature of your subject may well determine where you begin your research. A recent major event may require an initial search through the news outlets, whereas an historical theme may require you to start your search with specific books or websites.

If you are working in a group you will be able to gather information much faster than working alone. This may not always be possible, but if you do know the actors who will be performing your verbatim piece, this is an excellent opportunity for them to get involved.

*HINT: The more knowledgeable your actors are on the subject of your play, the better. Whether in verbatim theatre or not, an actor needs to have a solid understanding of the world and context in which the play is set; however, the need for this is even more acute with a verbatim piece.*

THE RESEARCH

### Activity: Research Topics

○ *Divide and conquer*   Divide your subject into smaller research topics. Assign one or more topics to each member of the company. Alternatively, it may be preferable to work in pairs.

○ *Two-minute presentations*   Sharing the information is the quickest way for the whole group to become as expert as each other. Insist that the presentations are short and concise.

*HINT: The aim of this is to gain the broadest possible knowledge of the subject matter. This foundation will then help you decide what aspects are most interesting or warrant further investigation.*

**Pre-Loaded** *devised by Robin Belfield & cast*
*College of Richard Collyer, Horsham (2015)*

*Pre-Loaded* was a verbatim project developed with a group of college students in West Sussex.

'Pre-loading' is the term used when young people drink a substantial amount of alcohol at home prior to a night out. The main reason for doing this was clear: with a limited amount of disposable income, they could buy alcohol cheaper at the supermarket and therefore have to buy less in expensive bars and clubs. But with only a small amount of research we discovered that there were other reasons too, that weren't just simply prudent or thrifty economics; it was fast becoming a culture. For example, many of the young women interviewed preferred to spend longer getting ready as a group, drinking as they did so and then wouldn't 'go out' until much later in the evening.

With this subject it didn't seem appropriate to divide into research topics, the subject itself is fairly easy to understand. The group was drawn to 'pre-loading' as a subject because it was relevant to their own lives as young people and students. 'Pre-loading' had also recently made the news, having been identified as an issue with young people and was being blamed as a significant contributing factor in an increase in young people's drinking and antisocial behaviour. So the primary aim of the research was to uncover the following:

- The facts and statistics.
- The opinions both for and against it.
- The associated effects or consequences – both positive and negative.

It therefore seemed most appropriate that each group was given the above list as headings to research, but was also given different source materials to search from.

THE RESEARCH

- Newspapers and magazines.

- Internet news pages.

- Social media.

*NB. It could have easily been conducted the other way round, i.e. each group was given just ONE of the headings in the first list, and were free to use any of the sources listed in the second list.*

## Getting the Most from Your Research

Gathering this initial research takes time. Don't short-cut! Gaps in your knowledge will only result in you having to go back and check your sources again or, worse yet, your final piece appearing ill-informed to the audience. Here are the essentials for collating the research and getting the most out of it:

*Spread your net wide*

During the process of creating verbatim theatre you will constantly be editing and removing things you don't want in order to keep the things you do; this constant distillation of material means you have to have enough to start off with – start with too little and it will quickly evaporate to nothing. The wider your initial research, the more likely you are to make richer discoveries – **the richer the discoveries, the better material, and the better the material, the better the play.** It's as simple as that!

*Start with the obvious*

Follow the clearest, strongest leads first, making sure you have all the basics covered. This is where you become a mini-expert. A significant part of his preparation for *The Power of Yes* for David Hare was first to understand completely the world of banking and the financial services. Without putting in the requisite spade-work, he wouldn't have begun to understand the information given by his interviewees as they attempted to explain what went wrong. Don't forget, what may seem obvious to you may not be to your audience; best at this stage not to take any knowledge for granted.

## Follow all the leads

Like any good detective, you have to follow where the leads take you. As you do, new and more unexpected avenues will almost certainly become apparent to you and require further investigation. As you follow these, they'll either lead you onwards to even more uncharted territory or back round to more familiar ground.

## Get organised

It won't take long before the amount of research you have collected begins to mount up, so keep it organised! You may choose to arrange it all into suitable categories, by date or some other way – as long as you are able to access the information quickly. There's nothing worse than getting halfway through the process and remembering a particular quote or statistic that would be ideal only to then not be able to find it!

## Make notes

Perhaps the most obvious pointer in this list, but get out the highlighter and red pen so, as you gather information, you can mark the things that strike you, ready for future reference. It may also help to summarise long documents or passages, or make brief reference notes at the top of the page.

## Develop your system

Every practitioner works differently. It's important that you quickly develop a way of working that suits you, your company and your project. How you search for and store the research is up to you, so long as you are able to refer back to and cross-reference information you require with ease.

## Share the knowledge

Even if you are working alone at this stage, there will come a point where you will need to share the information. It is of little use if it's all stored in your head, and the sheer amount of it will soon become overwhelming. Remember, you will ultimately have to share it with an audience, so regularly report back research findings to your colleagues – the better informed they are, the better equipped they will be to help you achieve a clear and engaging piece of theatre.

# Preparing for Your Interviews

The quality of your interviews will have a direct relationship to the quality of your verbatim piece; no matter how you edit it, dress it or sell it, there is no substitute for good material. There is an investigatory nature to verbatim theatre, constantly questioning and searching for the evidence that will make the point and prove the fact. Returning to my detective metaphor, you need to make sure you have gathered enough evidence (and hard evidence at that). You will have done a lot of this already in your research, covered all the bases, left no stone unturned – the clichés could go on! Now you need to draw up a list of your key witnesses. It is from their testimony that you will create this play. Of course statistical facts, quotes from the press, or social-media comments will always be useful, but these are secondary sources; chances are they won't provide you with enough material (or evidence) and you'll need to gather primary source material to present your case.

# Identifying the Voices

From your research you will have gained both a broad knowledge of the subject matter and also been able to investigate some of the detail. The next step is to pursue your strongest leads and interview them. You will need to identify the people whose voices need to be heard or who can provide you with information that you may be missing.

## Activity: Cast List

Look back over your research and identify those individuals whose names can be identified as having a **key voice**, **strong opinions** or indeed an **alternative perspective** on this subject. Once you have listed them, arrange them into the following categories:

○ **Witnesses** – *those who were there*
  These are the people who saw it, or experienced it first-hand. This testimony is the most valuable to a verbatim practitioner, as it is the closest you will get to the event itself.

○ **Experts** – *those who have professional interest*
  These are the professional people who can give you a deeper insight into the facts and figures. They are often one step removed from the event in terms of its context or emotional connection, but offer a wider outlook on the story. Your list of 'experts' may include one or more of the following:

  • Emergency services personnel (although if they were 'at the scene', these would also be classified as witnesses).
  • Politicians and leaders (local, national or even international).
  • Historians.
  • Government departments (such as Social Services).
  • Professionals or service providers (those who perhaps were not involved directly, but have a professional connection and authority: psychiatrists, youth workers, clergy, for example).

○ **Corporate** – *those with a financial or business interest*
Through your research you may have found names of
companies and organisations associated with your subject,
rather than individuals. It may be you can get access to the
owner or chief executive (or equivalent) for an official response,
but often a spokesperson is quoted on behalf of the company,
rather than a named person.

○ **Family and Friends** – *those connected to the witnesses*
In the instance of them not being witness to the event
themselves, they may still be able to provide valuable material
about your witnesses – their character, background and lifestyle.
They might also be able to provide an insight into how the event
has changed or affected the life or behaviour of a witness.

○ **General Public** – *those not listed above!*
You may well have chosen a subject that evokes strong
reactions from the public, especially those stories focused round
a local event. You may find it useful to try and gain a sense of
public opinion – in fact you may feel it's essential that the
general public are represented. However, while their opinions
may be interesting or provocative, it's essential to remember that
they are neither witnesses nor experts and therefore are simply
expressing opinion. That's not to lessen the value of or interest in
their interviews necessarily; it's just worth bearing in mind.

*HINT: Every verbatim play will be different and so you may
need to find different ways to categorise your interviewees.
The intention of these exercises is to ensure you have a
balance of voices that suits the needs of your play and the
story you have chosen to tell.*

## Activity: The Target Board

Taking your list of potential interviewees, you will need to start making
some initial judgements, in order to decide where to start with your
interviews. Another way of looking at it is to ask yourself: 'who do you
consider to be lead voices and who are supporting voices?' (I am

deliberately trying to avoid calling them 'characters' as that term carries with it the connotations of being fictitious.)

Rather than just reordering the list of names, I encourage verbatim practitioners to create a target board instead. It may not be easy (or even appropriate) to force your interviewees list into numerical order. The target board enables you to group interviewees visually according to how central you feel their voices are to the subject.

○ *Create your target board*   Either on the floor or on a wall, create a target board, similar to the diagram below.

○ *Gather the names of interviewees together*   Using sticky notes, or something similar, write each of the interviewees' names on a separate note.

○ *Arrange the names on the board*   Place each name onto the target. The more central you feel their voice is to the subject, the more central a placement you give them.

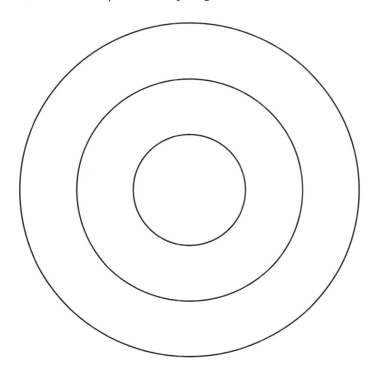

### Activity: For or Against?

You will have no doubt discovered, as the old saying goes, 'there are two sides to every story.' From your research, can you identify the strongest voices for each side?

○ *Divide your target*   Simply draw a line down the centre of your target board, one side labelled as 'For' and the other 'Against'.

○ *Reshuffle the names*   Shift the names so they are all on the appropriate side. Remember to keep them in the same zone on the target as you had previously identified in the earlier step.

○ *For*   The people offering a supportive or positive voice towards whatever event, decision, action that has sparked this conflict or debate.

○ *Against*   Those on the other side, with negative opinions against the event, decision or action.

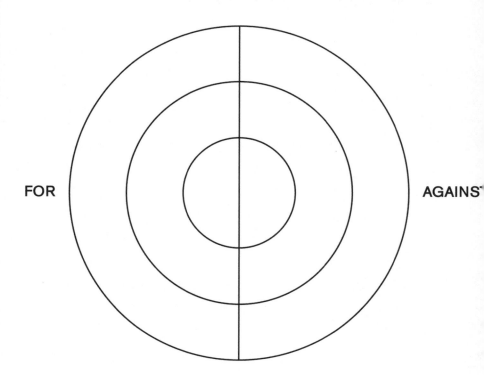

FOR

AGAINST

*HINT: It may not be possible to be as clear cut as 'For' or 'Against', and therefore you may wish to organise your target board into more than two points of view.*

○ *Divide your target further*   Remove all the name labels from your target board and then simply divide the circle into as many portions as you need (see diagram below).

○ *Reshuffle*   You can now reshuffle your names into the appropriate segments. In the diagram below I have illustrated a suggested division of the target based on family relationships. You will of course label these segments as appropriate to your subject.

**CHILDREN**

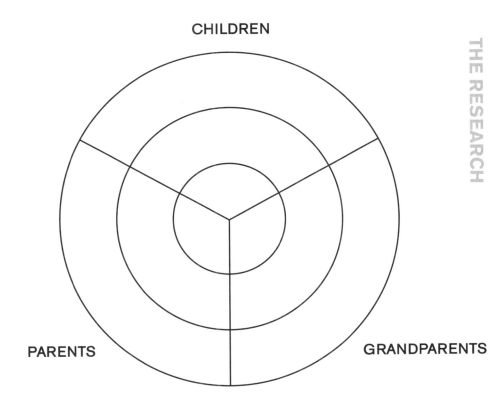

**PARENTS**

**GRANDPARENTS**

○ *Voice map*   Your target board is now a quick visual guide to the potential voices in your verbatim play, mapped out clearly in groups, which will help you prioritise your interviews.

○ *Quick reference*   Keep this target somewhere you can easily refer back to it. It may be that you want tick them off as you complete the interviews, or strike them through if you are not able to make contact or if they are not willing to take part.

*HINT: Of course you are not bound by the value judgements and the decisions you make at this stage. Every interview you conduct has the potential to surprise you with opinions you weren't expecting, or a point of view you hadn't considered before.*

The amount of research you are likely to generate is huge, so this exercise is a useful way of prioritising your time; for example, those people you identify at this stage as 'central' characters are the ones worth interviewing first. As a verbatim practitioner you will constantly be making these value judgements on the material you are collating, but you must remain open to the possibility of discovery and reassess your judgements at each stage. With each stage of this process you will gain a clearer insight and greater knowledge – it may be that you need to reshuffle the names again as you proceed.

## Approaching Interviewees

You have compiled your initial list of voices and organised them using the target boards; now you will need to start the sometimes long and arduous process of approaching the individuals to invite them to talk to you. Here are a few guidelines and things to remember, most of which are common sense but can easily be overlooked.

## Organise yourself

You will have a good start on this, having already organised your research, and now the target board can help you prioritise your list of names and identify the most central voices – those you need to approach first.

## Allow plenty of time

Be realistic about the responses you will receive – most people are not going to respond straight away. There are many reasons why they may be reluctant to speak to you: it might be because they don't understand or because the subject is difficult to talk about; it might simply be because they are busy and you are not high on their list of priorities.

## Make direct contact

Your first approach is likely to be an email or a phone call; try to make direct contact with your intended interviewee. This may be straightforward if you are interviewing peers at school or college, but not so easy when dealing with businesses, organisations and the authorities. You may have to do a little more research to find the right person to help you. An email sent to a generic company address is very likely to be overlooked, ignored or just dismissed.

## Be persistent

You will need to be prepared to follow up your initial approach perhaps several times. It's a fact of life that messages get lost, don't get passed on or sit in an inbox (or junk folder), so try and reach them by alternative means. Persistence is essential; it's highly unlikely you will get positive responses from every interviewee every time. But always be sensitive – there is a significant difference between being gently persistent and hassling people.

## Be prepared for refusal

They just might, so be prepared for it and accept it. Is there someone else who may offer a similar voice (another witness or expert)? Sometimes a 'no comment' response or a flat refusal to talk to you may work to your advantage, and may speak volumes in your verbatim play.

## Be polite

Your job is to encourage them to talk, to open up and to share. Sometimes this involves sharing personal or sensitive information and experiences. It's important your (potential) interviewees realise you respect that. It may sound obvious but they are more likely to agree to speak if you are being respectful and courteous.

## Be clear

Right from the start, outline what you are doing and why you want to speak to them. Let them know why it is important that they share their story with you. Also be clear about how you intend to use their interview. We will discuss the issues with ethics and verbatim theatre later (Chapter Six), but I can't think of many situations where material should be gathered by deception.

## Find the right venue

In many cases this will be obvious. Always make the effort to go to them rather than force them to travel to you. The comfort of familiar surroundings (their home or place of work) may prove the best environment for the interviewee to feel comfortable and confident that this interview is 'on their terms'. However, it may be that a more neutral location would be more appropriate. Make a suggestion, but check that they are okay with it and be open to them changing their minds. The venue and the circumstances of where and when the interview takes place may prove more than just convenience. It may also help feed your ideas later on when it comes to staging this play

– is the venue key to the person? Does the environment support or detract from the testimony they offer?

## Confirm arrangements

Don't waste an opportunity to speak to someone because it wasn't clear what the arrangements were – time, place, if they were going to bring something to show you, etc. Don't waste your time or theirs.

## Decide whether to name or keep anonymous

Identify early on whether they are happy to be named in the performance, explain to them what that means if they are unsure. They may prefer to remain anonymous and need to be reassured that you will protect their identity, perhaps by changing their name in the play. Be mindful of the fact that it might still be possible to identify someone without giving their name. We've all played the party games where we've had to guess a famous person, from clues about their identity, so double-check for any of these clues in their interview that might make anonymity difficult.

> HINT: If you promise anonymity make sure you honour that promise. Make a clear note somewhere so this instruction is not lost over time or by passing material to different company members and colleagues. You may choose to remove their name from recordings and transcripts immediately, in order to ensure their identity remains unknown.

# Recording

The dictionary definition of verbatim is '*in exactly the same words as were used originally*'.[3] Therefore it is essential you make clear and detailed records of your interviews. It's so easy with any mobile device to record the interview, and this is likely to be the quickest

3. *Concise Oxford English Dictionary*, twelfth edition (Oxford University Press, 2011).

and most effective method, but have a backup just in case. Batteries fail, digital memory is full, equipment gets lost or broken – it happens – so make sure you are prepared.

## Make notes

Even if you are recording, make detailed notes of the interview (including date, time and location where the meeting took place).

## Charge your battery

Or make sure you have an alternative power source! Voice recordings will use a lot of battery on most devices, and it's always hard to know how long each interview will take.

## Download previous material

Not only will it safeguard against running out of memory mid-interview, downloading each interview onto a computer hard drive will ensure your material is backed up, in case anything should happen to your recording device. Many modern devices will allow you to email voice memos straight back to yourself.

## Practise

If you've never recorded and/or transcribed an interview before, it's probably not the best idea for your interview with a key voice to be your first time. Practise with your colleagues, or anyone else who'll help. It doesn't matter what you talk about, pick an easy topic, one you know will get them talking (see pages 46–47 for an activity to assist with this).

## Label everything clearly

All the notes, transcripts and digital files that you amass need to be labelled with all the relevant information: names, dates, locations and any other information. *Again it is important you also make notes on any details that need to be kept confidential and not used or mentioned in your edit.*

> HINT: Your interviews are the most valuable resource you have, so it is vitally important that you protect them.

# In Discussion

## ACH Smith on Interview Technique

*ACH Smith is a Bristol-based writer. He started his career as a journalist and theatre critic. For ten years he interviewed actors and directors, and wrote editorials for the Royal Shakespeare Company's production programmes.*

*Over his long career he has written novels, poetry and plays, several of which investigate the history and culture of Bristol. Through this book we will have a chance to take a closer look at his two most popular plays* (Up the Feeder, Down the 'Mouth *and* Walking the Chains) *both of which use verbatim material. However, in this chapter it's his experience of conducting interviews that is most relevant to us, and here he shares some of his insights and advice about how to make the most of an interview.*

RB: *When researching* Up the Feeder... *and* Walking the Chains, *how did you select people to interview?*

ACHS: Both times I started by taking advice from an insider. On *Up the Feeder...*, a local journalist friend of mine who had covered Bristol Dock stories for years gave me the contacts for a couple of old dockers he knew who would tell me stories. From there, it went exponentially: every docker I talked to would say: 'you ought to talk to Bert/Fred/Harry', etc. I wound up talking to some fifty-odd dockers and seamen, and even then there were more I could have contacted, but enough was enough. For *Walking the Chains* it was more direct. I simply wanted to talk to a selection of the blokes currently working on maintaining Clifton Suspension Bridge, and the Visitor Centre staff suggested the most experienced ones and made the appointments for interviews.

*From your experience as a journalist, did you ever have to interview someone who was very reluctant, and how did you convince them to meet with you?*

As a journalist, yes, very occasionally someone would be reluctant, and you have to do your best to persuade them that information from them would serve a purpose to which they had some commitment. The same would apply in the case of seeking verbatim material for a play, but in practice I have never met any resistance. People are tickled by the idea that their words might be performed for an audience. You hope that in the course of the interview your manner will convince them that you do not have any fell intent, you are not going to misrepresent or ridicule them.

In TV filming, the producer brings out a consent form for the interviewee to sign. No such legal safeguards were ever observed in my newspaper and theatre experience. You just have to make sure that the people you interview understand why you want to hear what they have to tell you. And, of course, you offer them a couple of complimentary tickets to the show!

*What do you do in order to prepare for an interview?*

In journalism you usually know what the 'story' is – that is why you wanted the interview, to hear it in their words. In TV, particularly, I always had a list of questions prepared, to avoid the risk of drying on air. Every day you can see a TV interview which sticks to prepared questions, and it will not be engaging for the audience – you strive, rather, to make it feel like a conversation, and will digress from your line of questioning if something takes you by surprise, or delight.

For a play, it is the opposite. You want stories that you don't already know. So you start by asking a quite banal question – 'how did you get started in this job?', for example – and if you can create a friendly, conversational atmosphere, and show genuine interest in the subject, it won't be long before the interviewee goes into anecdotes. Then you just have to keep them going with responsive questions, which requires that you have been listening attentively.

*Do you have any advice or guidance on how to get the most out of your interviewee?*

Attend to what they are telling you. While the interview lasts, they are the only thing on your mind. It takes an effort of concentration, and so is more tiring for you than an ordinary conversation. But although you are working hard, you don't want to sound intense, which could clam them up; something like relaxed concentration is what you are after, just like an actor or a cricketer.

*What happens if you find the answers offensive or deceitful?*

If someone were to make, say, a racist remark, you can't get into an argument, this is not the time for it, but you can just tactfully let them know that you take another view, and move on. In some plays you might want to quote the offensive remark, trusting that the structure of the play will place it in context. The same would apply to deceit: it could be a telling line in the play, providing that you equip the audience to spot it for what it is.

*How would you approach pursuing a line of questioning that might be particularly sensitive or emotional?*

It is extraordinary where a conversation can take you. I began talking to a suspension-bridge maintenance man about the mechanics of his job, and suddenly, unprompted, he was telling me about the traumatic experience of dealing with people who are on the bridge in order to jump off it and kill themselves. Clearly it was a profound part of the job he did, and he wanted to share it with someone who would understand him. That I might retell the story on stage was not

THE RESEARCH

on his mind. It was what he wanted me to know. I got his express permission to use the words.

If your interview touched on, say, a recent bereavement, the interviewee would most likely have known it would when they agreed to meet you and be recorded, so they should be emotionally prepared for it. All you need is the sympathy you would have if it came up when talking to someone in a pub. You use your decency to judge how far to press them for what might be painful details. You can't make rules on this. For some people, talking about it could be cathartic.

I was interviewing an eighty-year-old retired docker and suddenly he mentioned his father, who had also been a docker, and then he broke down in sobs. I kept quiet while he recovered, assuming that he was still grieving for his father's death. I was wrong. The sobs were over the industrial injustice that his father had suffered. By the time I had learned the whole story, and done my research, I had a moving new play on my hands, now written but not yet produced.

*Do you have a preferred method to take a record of an interview? Do you take notes during the interview in shorthand? Or do you use a Dictaphone and transcribe it later?*

I don't have shorthand. I used to scribble notes in my version of speed-hand, and trust my memory to resurrect phrases when I got back to my desk. Now I use a Dictaphone, preferably with a clip-on mic on the interviewee. They never seem to feel self-conscious about being recorded. They just get into talking to you.

*How far do you go to protect the anonymity of the interviewee? When is it appropriate to use someone's real name?*

The first time I wrote a play using verbatim was *Prostitutes* (an adaptation of Jeremy Sandford's book, commissioned by Tony Robinson's Avon Touring Company in 1976). I interviewed several women 'on the game', including the local officer of their embryonic trade union, who was my source for contacts. I didn't think it appropriate to use

THE RESEARCH

their real names but, as they often do in their line of work, gave them false names on stage. The next verbatim job, in Chichester, was about the Battle of Britain, when I interviewed several veteran fighter pilots. They were only too happy to be named in the script. After that, in 1985 there was a partly verbatim play about the Great Western Railway for the Bristol Old Vic, called *God's Wonderful Railway*, and again there was no problem in using real names. In *Up the Feeder...* I used the wonderful nicknames that all the dockers gave each other.

For *Walking the Chains* I had a slightly tricky problem. Apart from the Bridge Master, whom I named by his job title, the men I interviewed all did the same work, or, now tollbooth keepers, were superannuated from that work, and so much of what they told me overlapped. Hence, it was not always expedient to be strict in allocating verbatim quotes to the character who had actually spoken the words. So I spread the quotes among them according to the dramatic requirements, and thus thought it wrong to use proper names, since each character was something of an amalgam. I made up names for them.

○    ○    ○

## Transcribing the Interviews

Once you have conducted an interview, if you are following the 'recorded delivery' method you'll need to be able to find a way of editing the audio files before sharing with your actors (see Chapter Four on this method, and Chapter Five for guidance on how to select which lines to keep and which to remove). Most likely, however, you'll need to transcribe the interview onto paper so you can edit and shape as part of your script.

Transcription is another element that gets easier with practice. Be under no illusion, this is where verbatim work gets *really* time-consuming; endlessly playing and replaying short clips of audio in order to transcribe the words exactly. It's important at this stage that you are not tempted into editing as you go along, rather transcribe the interview in full and then you can think about what you might want to remove. The remaining activities and provocation in this chapter will be best done with the whole text under scrutiny.

Not only will you have to write down every word, you must also find a way of transcribing what's *not* said. In a traditional fictional play script, the stage directions can provide useful hints to the actor, especially on first reading, how the playwright imagines the lines being spoken. Here you have to be more specific and give as clear instructions and guidance as you can. Noting each pause is probably the most obvious example. But you'll soon realise that real speech is much more difficult to write down than made-up speech. People stop mid-sentence, change topic without warning, interrupt their own thoughts as well as other people's... I could go on. As you proceed you'll need to settle on a simple system that you can keep consistent across all your interviews. The more information you can give the actor, the more able they will be to reproduce the speech as close to the original as possible.

There is more guidance on 'laying out your script' in Chapter Seven, but if you can establish a clear system early on with your transcripts, you save time later down the line.

## Whose Agenda?

Once you have gathered together your interviews, it is worth investigating the interviewee's **agenda**. It may be directly linked to their opinions as you already understand them; however, it may not be as straightforward as that. After some further thinking, you may wish to reassess their testimony within the context of your play. It could be argued that verbatim theatre is the most objective of theatre genres and it is of course *capable* of total impartiality. As a verbatim practitioner you have an opportunity to present both sides of a story, or reflect all angles and opinions – if you choose to! Throughout this process (and this handbook), your value judgements will be called into question – your decisions about who to interview, what to edit out, and ultimately what makes it onto the stage will all demonstrate *your* opinions and *your* agenda.

Let's not pretend your agenda doesn't exist, or attempt to hide behind a false sense of fairness. Being aware of it and honest about it is the only way to keep it under control. And not only that, but you will also need to heighten your awareness of other people's agendas. **EVERYONE HAS AN AGENDA.** Every article, every book, every expert, every witness will express their own point of view. It may be strikingly obvious or it may be hidden; either way your job is to be aware of it, always. That way, you can make appropriate choices at the various stages of the process, by either exploiting that particular agenda or by ensuring it's balanced with opposing ones.

You have already made assumptions about this on your target board (pages 24–28). By placing the names on either the 'for', 'against', or the other defined groupings, you have begun to assess or judge their opinions. Your judgement of them may alter slightly as you conduct your interviews. But you cannot alter someone's agenda – in many cases they may not be aware of it themselves.

### *Activity: Uncovering Intentions*

A well-used technique for actors and directors is to examine a character's **intentions** or **objectives** – in other words, asking what it is this character wants to *do*, or *achieve*, by saying those lines at that moment. This can be a really useful activity for the verbatim practitioner to do with interviewees whose voices will be included in the play.

○ *Listen*   Re-listen or re-read over an interview at least a couple of times.

○ *Identify the intention*   Why did they agree to speak to you? What do they hope to achieve by answering your questions? Imagine yourself in their shoes and ask yourself: 'with this interview I want to…'

Possible answers might include:

- Make my voice heard.
- Protect my reputation (or that of someone else, whether personal or corporate).
- Get some publicity (or raise profile, whether personal or for my company/organisation).
- Show my support (for the subject or a witness).
- Fight my corner.

○ *Rate the strength of their agenda* Again, in order to create a balanced piece, you may wish to include testimony from those with very strong opinions as well as those who may be milder in their approach. When it comes to piecing testimonies together to form the play's structure, you will need to consider the tempo, pace and shape of the story as it develops (more on this in Chapter Four). A simple colour-coding system is a great way to rate the strength of an agenda clearly:

- *Red*: strong, perhaps even vehement in their opinions, keen to impress their clear agenda.
- *Green*: clear in their opinions but more balanced in their statements.
- *Blue*: cool or indifferent to any opinion. This may also mean they are shy, anxious or reluctant to express it honestly.

Place a sticker of the appropriate colour on the interviewee's name, as a quick guide you can refer back to at a later stage.

*HINT: This work may well come in useful later on when working with the actors during rehearsals. When they have been cast, you may set them this challenge to specify their characters' agenda or 'intentions'.*

## Group Interviews

One-to-one interviews may not be possible and won't always be the best method to gather the material you are after. Extremely useful when dealing with sensitive subjects, they do allow you to build trust with interviewees and gather the thoughts and insights that might not be expressed in a more open forum; however, it can feel a little formal and interviewees might feel (especially if they are being recorded) as though they are being put on the spot.

In these circumstances it may be best to conduct a group interview. How many of us have been only too happy to share our moans or misgivings in a social environment (the staff canteen or in the pub), but when asked directly in a more formal setting we clam up, not willing to get down from the fence? The group chat often facilitates a more open conversation, especially on subjects that affect everyone in the group. They can respond to each other, which means you as the interviewer are able to be a less prominent presence, able to listen to where the conversation leads rather than feeling obliged to lead it.

I always remember the *Creature Comforts* animations as a prime example of this. These originated in the late eighties with a short film by Nick Park and Aardman Animations (who went on to create Wallace and Gromit), which used the verbatim voice recordings of the general public being interviewed on various domestic subjects. Their voices were then given to animated animals. In several cases it was a group of family members or friends, and the choice of animals (a family of polar bears or a flock of birds) and the resulting animation reflected the dynamic of the voices and the group – interrupting each other, talking over each other, finishing each other's sentences and so on – giving just as much, if not more, insight into the group as the words themselves.

However you gather the material, do not be tempted to rush this part of the process. Most verbatim practitioners, certainly the ones mentioned in this book, would agree that this takes time, and time taken to be careful and thorough is time well spent. Poor-quality research and material will not only do you and your play a disservice, but also undermines the integrity of the voices you seek to represent.

# 3. ■ The Words

## *How to prepare to tell your own story*

What if you are the subject, or stand at the centre of it? What if it's your experiences or eyewitness account that needs to be voiced? You may not need to seek the voices and opinions of other people, and the idea of conducting an interview with yourself feels faintly ridiculous. This of course is another variant of verbatim theatre and many of the techniques are directly applicable. Likewise, so are the responsibilities; you must do yourself the courtesy of being respectful of what may be a difficult or sensitive issue; equally, you must also ensure you are able to maintain a certain amount of detachment.

### *Check your agenda*

Why do you need to give this subject a platform, and, indeed, is this the right platform for it?

### *Timing*

Why now? Go back to the Important/Urgent Axis (Chapter One), but also acknowledge that now there is a personal connection you need to be sure that you are ready to investigate and perhaps even interrogate your own thoughts, feelings and actions.

*Yourself as subject and storyteller*

Are you the right person to tell your story? Or would it have a stronger impact if you handed that responsibility to someone else – another practitioner, a colleague, or members of your company?

# Generating Your Own Material

## *In a Group*

The decision to generate your own material may be less emotional and more practical when you are working as a group – a class or an ensemble responding with a collective connection to the subject rather than an individual one.

When leading courses on making verbatim theatre, I start as described by looking for the subject and, when working with students, this will often end up being something that is close to home. Take *Pre-Loaded* (see page 19–20) as a case in point. The issue of 'pre-loading' (drinking significant amounts of alcohol before a night out, where even more drinking will happen), was something they all had experiences of and opinions about. In circumstances like this, I have been required to creates a complete (albeit short) piece of verbatim theatre to perform at the end of the series of workshops. When there is only a limited amount of time, and/or the subject matter has a direct connection to the group, it makes practical sense that we start with the 'experts' we have in the room and for the group to produce its own material (or at least some of it).

## *Activity: The Spectrum Debate*

○ *Set out the spectrum*   Establish that one end of the room represents the response: 'strongly agree'. The other end of the room therefore represents the opposite response: 'strongly disagree'.

○ *Mark the 'fence'*   Establish for the group where the halfway point between the two extremes is and mark it as the 'fence', on which no one is allow to sit! They can be as close to it as they like, but *must* fall on one side or the other.

○ *Set the statement*   Give the group a clear statement relating to your chosen subject. It's important that it's a statement and not a question, e.g. 'Fox hunting should be made legal again' rather than 'Should fox hunting be made legal again?'

○ *Set the ground rules*   While they are thinking about their response to the statement, it might be beneficial to establish some simple ground rules; things like:

1. We will all be open-minded to different responses.
2. This is a safe space, we are free to speak our opinions without being judged.
3. Everyone can change their minds.

And so on.

○ *Place yourself on the spectrum*   Ask the group to place themselves physically in the space according to how strongly they 'agree' or 'disagree', making sure no one sits on the fence.

○ *Let the debate begin*   You might want to start with those at the extreme, asking them to explain why they placed themselves at this particular place on the spectrum.

○ *Hear from everyone*   If you don't have time to speak to everyone, make sure you facilitate both sides of the argument with an equal opportunity to speak. Remember, people may be stood next to each other on the spectrum (essentially with the same opinion therefore), but have very different reasons for that.

○ *Give the opportunity to move*   Like any good debate, we have the power to change minds and allow our own mind to change.

THE WORDS

After hearing the arguments, give everyone ten seconds to reassess their position on the spectrum. How has the shape of the spectrum changed? Ask what made people change their minds.

○ *Don't forget to record the responses*   However you do it, if this debate is to provide you with source material, you have to make sure you record it so you can transcribe and capture the thoughts and opinions. *Make sure everyone is aware you are recording and happy to take part.*

### *Activity: Interview Each Other*

○ *Plan*   Assuming you have established your subject, individually plan a few starter questions.

   *HINT: Stick to open-ended questions; the idea is to try and not lead them towards answers you think you'll hear or that you* want *to hear.*

○ *Pair up*   Keep a good distance between pairs, or move to separate spaces if possible, so you aren't disturbed or distracted by other nearby conversations.

○ *Interview*   Keep it short at first, perhaps just a few questions. Remember your questioning is an attempt to allow the interviewee to open up and share their stories or experiences freely with you.

○ *Transcribe*   Are you able to transcribe or make notes quickly enough? Remember, your notes need to be more than just accurate, they must be verbatim.

○ *Record*   Although practising transcription and note-taking is very good experience, you'll stand a better chance of capturing every word if you record it and transcribe it later.

○ *Swap*   Swap over; now interviewer becomes interviewee. By the end everyone has contributed and together the group has collected a good amount of material.

This may only be the start, and you may find that even though the group are the 'witnesses' and the 'experts', you may still require further material to be gathered from external sources – other people, news sources and so on – to support or add balance to your own voices.

## On Your Own

So far, for the most part, I have assumed you are working as part of a group; however, you may well be approaching this verbatim play on your own and it is equally possible that you may be the subject, with your own personal experiences constituting the story.

This sense of autobiographical play would also fit within the spectrum of verbatim theatre, because it is not derived from the imagination, nor does it create a fictional representation of yourself. It remains utterly grounded in fact and truth – the only difference being that the play is created from *your* own original words, rather than from *theirs*.

**Groomed**, *written and performed by Patrick Sandford, Ingenious Purpose (2015)*

Writer and director Patrick Sandford developed this one-man play based on his own experiences of childhood abuse. The play tells Sandford's story of how, as a young schoolboy, he was groomed by a male teacher into an abusive relationship. Sandford is himself the storyteller and through the performance also plays his younger self and the teacher, accompanied by a single musician who underscores and punctuates the action.

The play's strapline is 'How can a Truth be told? How can a Secret be spoken?' which chimes with what is at the heart of verbatim theatre. Sandford's play takes us through the process of telling this truth, revealing the secret to the audience as his younger self is unable to disclose the abuse he is being subjected to. But it goes even deeper than a simple account of what happened, as he talks about his own sense of guilt and rejection that surrounded him as a boy, and the shame and anger felt through the subsequent years.

I think this is a particularly masterly example of autobiographic verbatim theatre that deftly walks the line between an honest, often deeply traumatic narrative, and the objectivity of a storyteller who is able to tell it with frank clarity. 'Honest and provocative – but never depressing' reads the show's marketing, and it's a very accurate description. The power of this play lies in the fact that it never descends into a tsunami of emotion – rage, despair, grief and so on. It contains all these, but with a level of restraint that makes it not simply bearable for the audience to watch, but deeply compelling.

## In Discussion

### *Patrick Sandford on Creating* Groomed

*Patrick Sandford is a writer and theatre director. Previously he was the Artistic Director at the Nuffield Theatre in Southampton, and prior to that at the Lyric Theatre in Belfast. He has written numerous plays and adaptations before forming a new theatre company, Ingenious Purpose, touring work across the UK and abroad.*

*RB: How did* Groomed *initially come about as a project? What drove you to write about your experiences?*

PS: I think there are two answers to that question. One is I left the Nuffield Theatre, which I had been running for twenty-something years; I knew I was leaving and I had realised to what extent the theatre had been a survival mechanism for me. A way of leading my life, let's not say avoiding other issues, but possibly *transforming* them. Having that recognition that it had served me so well (and then leaving it), really meant I was exposed to the history of my life (or the other part of my life), so I couldn't really avoid it. I also had time to look at it without the constraints of running the theatre, thinking: 'oh my God what will my board think? What will the audience think? What will my staff think?' So that's one answer. It needed to be done.

The other, I think, was that I reached an age in my life where I was understanding things in a more balanced way and feeling the need to express them, to speak about them. To that extent, it wasn't that I sat down and said: 'I am going to write this play', because in a very real sense the play wrote itself. People ask how long did it take to write and I say: 'well, fifty years!' Actually some of the material in it I wrote probably at least twenty years ago: maybe as scraps of writing in a book, or the back of an envelope, or maybe as a poem or as a journal entry. And when, a bit like coming out as gay, I thought it's about time I should talk about this, it was quite a natural thing for me to use the medium that was my profession, namely the theatre.

In 2012 I actually blagged my way onto a training event for counsellors and therapists who worked with survivors of abuse, in Scarborough, and they had this evening of 'creative expression' and I thought: 'well, I'll do a little bit of the stuff I've been writing.' The event was happening in a primary school and there were the little tables and stacks of those little chairs, and I have no idea why, but I just suddenly picked one up and I held it while I did some ten minutes of stuff. At the end, this woman, who was very experienced therapist, came up to me and said: 'where did you get the idea of that little chair? It was just utterly brilliant, so moving and powerful.' And I said: 'well, I didn't get the idea, I just picked it up!'[4] Their response to the work was so positive I thought: 'well, I've just got to do it' – I had no concept of *where* I was going to perform it, if I was *ever* going to perform it; it was like a sort of exercise to write it and I wrote it over the next two years.

4. A small school chair is one of the few but hugely significant props used in the final show.

First of all, I did it for my therapist who was retiring, and I thought I must do it for him before he retires. He went very quiet and after a long pause said: 'I'm not sure it's really West End material, but you have to do this, it's extraordinary.' So I hired a room at RADA, I did it for three friends in the morning, and three in the afternoon and they all said I had to keep working on it. A few months later, I did it to my agent who said: 'we'll get a wonderful actor to do it, you can't possibly do it yourself.' I then did it to the leadership team of a therapy school and immediately the chief therapist said: 'you have to do it yourself; it's a testimony.' And that was literally three or four hours after my agent had seen it so that was quite confusing. I was encouraged to apply to the Arts Council for some development money. That's when it became serious and I got Nancy Meckler [to direct] and Simon Slater to do the music.

So I did not sit down and say: 'I'm going to do a theatre piece about this'; it sort of emerged and I think that's quite important. The reason I think that's quite important is if you are writing your own stuff you have a choice: you can literally fictionalise it, and indeed I had written some short stories in which I called myself 'Paul'; but if you are going to write the *truth* and express it as yourself, the motivation has to be to write the truth, not to 'educate'. I say it in the programme, I wrote *Groomed* to tell the truth, to speak the truth, and perhaps to help myself understand it better and therefore help remove some of its power.

*So you have years and years' worth of material, can you tell me about the process you went through to shape it into a script?*

I went through my diary journals, and please don't believe this was an ordered thing, it wasn't! This was a jumble of stuff, not just at the bottom of a drawer, but in sixteen different places in the flat, literally on the back of envelopes, inside exercise books and things I'd scribbled down – so it was chaos! I went through it all and the stuff that was most vivid to me went in; and the stuff that I realised was more prosaic, I don't mean in terms of style but just that was more boring, middle-of-the-night depressive stuff that didn't have much universal significance, I left out. I very shambolically pulled it together into a sort of shape and then realised where the gaps were. Some of them were narrative gaps and some of them were more emotional gaps, and there I wrote additional truthful material from memory.

Once I got Nancy Meckler in, she started saying things like: 'you need to lead us in more gently, we need to get to know you a little bit more before you start on the really painful stuff.' So I wrote the stuff on King Midas as a sort of introduction, and that just came from my childhood memory. I remember reading the story about King Midas and his [secret donkey] ears, that was so vivid it just went in. Another thing Nancy said was: 'tell us more about the teacher before he starts abusing you.' So that's when I wrote the little bit about him teaching us handwriting, which he did. I wrote about twenty lines to give the impression of a teacher who is actually rather endearing and that the audience would want to like. I think the purpose of that was to make the experience easier for the audience, I genuinely don't think it was for some sort of shock effect. I think when writing truth, of course, my instinct as a showman and as a theatre-maker will sometimes take theatrical metaphor like the moment when I threw the chair across the room, which everyone finds rather shocking. But if you said to me: 'to what extent was that theatrical manipulation and to what extent did that emerge from the truth of the situation?' I'd be hard pushed to tell you which. But part of my 'truth' is making theatre; I don't think I ever deliberately said: 'right, I need a really theatrical moment here, let's do something theatrical.'

Incidentally, deciding to write about the handwriting presented me effortlessly with a simple and very useful theatrical device – the old-fashioned fountain pen. I hold it and gesture with it whenever I play the teacher. Rather like the little chair I did not need to think about this – it just happened.

Quite interestingly, Nancy quite early on in rehearsals said: 'it's really very difficult to criticise what you've written because it's the truth'; this was understandable but nonsense because it is this specific truth that I'm proposing to show to an audience (not everything about my life), so an element of creativity becomes involved. So immediately we're talking about the fact that verbatim theatre is the truth, but there is a selection process – a refining process: all the words on the page are my words but sometimes the way I have written it down is so self-indulgent, or naff, or long-winded, or just not very interesting, that I have to say to myself: 'could I say that in a more interesting way, in a more crystallised way?' I think brevity is so important, that became the most rigorous discipline – because I was so terrified that it was going to be a sort of self-indulgent agony-fest!

*I'm interested to know, apart from just keeping it short, how else did you mitigate against the play descending into an 'agony-fest'?*

When I was writing my notebooks twenty years ago clearly I wasn't mitigating anything, I was just writing, writing, writing. One of my favourite poets has always been Emily Dickinson, who is so brief as to be obscure sometimes, but who has the ability to crystallise emotion in very tight form. The playwright Racine wrote the most searing emotional stuff in rhyming alexandrines,[5] and Shakespeare does it in his great speeches too, it is all so rigorously controlled that the emotion can't sprawl. So my instinct was to compress, compress, compress.

The thing about verbatim theatre is that it's 'theatre', so there has to be an art form, which means you can't just splurge it all out. So you're making choices. I think the discipline has to be very, very strong when it is your own words. Now, when I went to write about the man abusing me in the classroom, the way I did that was I wrote a sonnet, I don't know if it's a very good sonnet and at that moment that didn't really matter, what mattered was that I was forcing myself to crystallise the experience and to contain it so that it wouldn't be too much or too long. There are lots of the other parts of the play that are similarly contained, even if they're not in the form of a sonnet, but I would say: 'I will not have more than three sentences here', or: 'this

5. The French 'alexandrine' was a form of poetic verse, typically the line would be made up of twelve syllables (as opposed to Shakespere's iambic pentameter that contains ten syllables).

sentence will not have so many adjectives or so many words.' I think that's just being creative, I suppose, and also being modest in a funny way – 'I will limit how much of this drivel comes out of my mouth.'

*You talked about the process of refining and editing, but how was it rehearsing with a director on your own material?*

I think what was interesting was how much time she spent asking me not to play the emotion at all. But simply to say the lines and allow the emotion to come up when it chooses to comes up. Where there were clearly lines of emotions like anger, she used to say to me: 'delay the anger for as long as you can.'

She made me action my script, in terms of what I was trying to do to the audience on every line, one after the other, which gave me the shifts of tone, of pace, of pitch. She did that a lot with the music – 'after that explosion of anger just stop and let the saxophone do the work and now start again on a completely different tone.' I would be aware quite often that I had written that different tone, but I wasn't necessarily playing it as sharply as I might have done because the previous tone leaked into what came next.

*Can you tell me a bit about performing it? What was it like to recount these personal experiences not in front of your friends or colleagues, but strangers – a paying audience?*

There is a certain anxiety that there might be some people who thought it was a heap of shite, or might mock me, or might not take me seriously, or get bored, or who fall asleep, or who go on their mobile phone, or might fidget and that I would find that distressing. To the best of my knowledge that never happened. Now I can't guarantee that, but certainly I could always hear a pin drop; I got people's attention. So that worry went away. Doing a one-person show is quite rigorous – there's no one else to take the energy, but I've been a director long enough to know that I have to deliver; there's no point coming and giving a half-cocked performance, I have to deliver the energy.

In the moment it's quite energising, the adrenaline flows and one feels quite good, as any actor does, you feel kind of seen and witnessed. In the short to medium term, afterwards, quite a big adrenaline slump, quite bad depression and an awareness of the truth of what I have spoken at a more profound level than before I spoke it. Longer term, it is immensely empowering and liberating because I think the speaking of any secret is ultimately freeing. It poses its own challenges – how much do I want my mother to see this piece? The answer is she knows I'm doing it, she knows what it's about, but I don't want her to see it in full. I don't feel the need to cause her distress – it's my stuff to sort out. Speaking the truth is liberating, but not always a pleasant experience. Then there's the big question of how having done it is going to change my life, the way I lead my life, the habits and thought-patterns of a lifetime. This is a challenge, but a good one.

I suppose the other thing that's quite interesting is that, because I have worked in theatres, I have been an artistic director, an awful lot of my creative work has been under somebody else's umbrella. The theatre company provides a structure. With *Groomed*, okay, I had the support of Kate Anderson and Ingenious Purpose (which we formed), but really I conceived, made and performed it for myself and by myself. For such a large project to be totally self-initiated was, for me, something a bit new. It tells me I could do it again if I want to. That's quite exciting.

*It's been a couple of years since its first public performance; has it changed much since then?*

One consequence of using my own words is that there is the potential for change to occur. As I understand more fully exactly what it is I am saying I can alter the text from performance to performance. I can also notice the effect on the audience and adjust. In *Groomed*, after many performances, I decided to add a scene in which the teacher, the perpetrator of the abuse, addresses the audience directly in an attempt to justify himself. This scene is clearly invented by me, but in writing it I used *verbatim* words I had heard spoken by paedophiles I had met, together with the *verbatim* words of a fellow pupil, a little girl, who I heard unforgettably speaking in the playground when I was ten years old. So this became 'verbatim theatre' within 'verbatim theatre'.

○   ○   ○

Working in this way certainly has its advantages, the main one being control over your voice and your artistry. But equally the demands are high too – as Sandford describes, an even greater level of discipline is required, in order to sense check and mitigate against that potential 'self-indulgent agony-fest'!

Sandford's description of his process makes it clear that, at some point, at some level, theatre always demands collaboration. Even his example, speaking his truth about something so personal, required the support and the assistance of others (essentially a director, a composer, a producer). It then becomes a question of deciding when is the right moment to bring them on board and, most important of all, who are the right people, those who you trust can help you tell your story, your truth as it needs to be told.

# 4. The Story

## How to uncover the story within the material

Within the mass of research and interview material is a **story** ready to be told. It may have already become clear to you, or it may still be waiting to be discovered. No doubt you will have become very familiar with all your research, if you are working as a group you may need to spend some time sharing and reporting back your findings (see Chapter Two for ideas on how to share your research).

I would argue that there is a difference between **narrative** and **story**. When I approach verbatim work, the 'narrative' for me is linked to the structure and can be defined or expressed as a series of events – what happens when. The 'story' is something more profound – it is a way of expressing what lies at the heart of the verbatim play. The structure of an event-based piece can be found very easily, but to simply perform a chronology of events would make for an 'interesting' audience experience at best. I can't imagine anyone walks into the theatre just to learn about a sequence of facts; on the contrary, an audience expects to be moved by connecting with the subject on a deeper level, so finding the story will help you achieve this.

Previously, we explored ways in which you can organise and categorise the material you have gathered. It is at this point in the process where the careful organisation of your research material will be of real value to you. Look for links between interviews – the recurring opinions will help you uncover what lies beneath the words. Also explore what has *not* been said; is there an unanswered question or indeed 'an elephant in the room'?

In Chapter One, when deciding on the subject of your verbatim piece, you invented titles for your ideas. A good title will both inform the potential audience what the play is about, and will suggest a deeper theme that they are being invited to explore. For example, Alecky Blythe and Adam Cork's *London Road* states the location of the play, following the news story that made the road infamous; but at the same time contains a subtext which relates to the theme of community. London Road is a residential street, and quite possibly one of the most common road names in the country, but the story at the heart of this play is how this community coped with adversity.

### Activity: Titles

○ Return to the titles you thought of for your chosen subject and discuss if they are still relevant. Are these still appropriate titles for the research you have found?

○ Are there new titles you can think of which would be more appropriate – that both inform and invite your potential audience?

## Approaching the Story

Different practitioners have different ways of approaching verbatim work. Here we take the opportunity to explore the processes of different practitioners, with reference to some specific work. It's worth noting here the use of the word 'practitioner', as most professional theatre-makers working with verbatim material act as both writer and director (and often performer as well). This is the case with both Ivan Cutting and Alecky Blythe, whom I have chosen to compare in this chapter, as both are extremely experienced practitioners, but approach verbatim work in quite different ways.

## Ivan Cutting: Artistic Director, Eastern Angles

Ivan Cutting formed Eastern Angles Theatre Company in 1982 as the regional touring theatre company for the East of England. Building on its origins as a rural touring company, it has developed a national reputation and expanded to tour work across the country. Ivan grew up in East Anglia and, although he trained at the University of Bristol, he returned to the region to form Eastern Angles whose work is deeply connected to the stories and communities of the area.

*Parkway Dreams* by Kenneth Emson
*Key Theatre Studio, Peterborough, then touring (2013)*

In the 1960s the population increase in the South East of England was becoming a major problem for the UK Government. The existing housing was in no way going to meet the needs of the rise. In London especially the available housing was quickly becoming cramped and unsanitary, therefore the Government looked to create 'New Towns' outside of London as a solution. In 1968 the expansion of Peterborough began and at the time it was the largest development of its kind – with the ambition to house 200,000 people.

*Parkway Dreams* incorporated material from many different sources and interweaved the history (and process) of the town's redevelopment, while at the same time exploring the personal experiences of families who had relocated from London.

It's a fascinating example of how verbatim and archive material can be gathered from a wide spectrum of sources, put together as a narrative, becoming more than 'documentary' but also satire, social drama and musical comedy. In his programme notes, director Ivan Cutting writes:

> *Parkway Dreams* may be the first musical about town planning! The show has been made up of a number of different elements. First there are the verbatim extracts from over a hundred different interviews, with people who worked for the Development Corporation, people who moved here, and people who watched it happen around them. Then there is the archive material that uncovered the plans for Queensgate, the arguments about demolition plans, and the inevitable jostling for best position amongst shops and local business. We supplemented this information with a trip to the National Archives in Kew and dug out the Ministry of Housing and Local Government, who piloted the expansion programme.

> To add a bit of nostalgia we added sketches based on the TV programmes and game shows of the time to satirise and sometimes simplify the arguments and debates of the time.

> With the addition of song-and-dance numbers that cut in and out of the scenes, we aimed to celebrate the sheer ambition of the development whilst also adding an element of fun and irreverence.

The **subject** here is the mass-building of new housing, but the **story** is in the personal experiences of a family moving into a 'new town'.

***Beyond the Breakers*** *by Ivan Cutting*
*The Seagull Theatre, Lowestoft (2005)*

This earlier play from Eastern Angles takes as its subject the lives and experiences of Norfolk lifeboatmen. The story charts the challenging transition from the instinctive knowledge and intuition of the local fisherman, to a world dominated by technology and health and safety regulations.

Defined by Ivan Cutting as more of a classic piece of 'documentary theatre', there is still an interesting interplay between the verbatim material and the 'play', i.e. an imagined narrative created by Cutting. In the programme for the production, he describes the process in more detail:

> It's like two plays crammed into one: there is the documentary material and the play. The documentary sections were produced from oral-history interviews, archive material and book research. This involved many trips up to North Norfolk to interview lifeboatmen, old and new, and then long hours meticulously transcribing their accounts and then editing them down into scenes; rummaging through books and newspaper accounts of past rescues and launches; and combing through the archives for details of one of the many lifeboat disasters, like that in Wells in 1880. All of these documentary sections are based on actual words of those who were witness to the events and should have the distinct flavor of actuality. And then operating in parallel to this is a play, which I have written, with fictional characters, plot and story, although very much set in Sheringham now. It is based on the experiences as I saw them of the modern lifeboat crew and more recent events. I must emphasise this 'as I saw them' because, although the play too is based on those interviews and research, it has a different relationship to them. It is not actual truth but fictional truth and investigates different areas of the modern lifeboat world. It is especially difficult precisely because of its close connection with a known locality.

These two plays by the same company, offer examples of different ways in which verbatim material can be used to create a story. Both these examples of Ivan Cutting's work and the process he describes combine fact with fiction. The authenticity of the documentary elements validates and adds credence to an imagined narrative and characters. It is similar to the work we have previously explored by ACH Smith (*Walking the Chains* and *Up the Feeder...*), with the slight difference that Smith's dramatisation is predominantly the imagined dialogue of the past and the modern text is constructed from the verbatim material. Instead, Cutting, perhaps because he is dealing with more recent events, utilises his oral history as verbatim text and dramatises the modern scenario to give the play a narrative structure.

## In Discussion

### Ivan Cutting on His Plays and Practice

*RB: Can you tell me a little of how you were introduced to verbatim theatre?*

IC: I was very influenced by the work of Peter Cheeseman. I saw *The Knotty* back in 1966 and thought it was fantastic and exactly the kind of theatre I wanted to make. So when we started Eastern Angles, the first show I directed was a musical documentary of the Lowestoft herring-fishing industry, all done to strict Cheeseman rules where you had to have a 'primary source witness' for everything you put on. We used extensive oral-history interviews with the old fishermen to tell our story.

*What gave you the idea to write a play about Peterborough?*

We were asked to go to Peterborough to do some work since the city was classed as having a 'low cultural offer' by the Arts Council – indeed, it didn't have a single Arts Council-funded organisation in a city of 200,000. Although a city, it was also a New Town, transformed by a massive development programme from 1968–88. At first we found it was very different to the rural places we'd worked before. But we thought we should do exactly the same as we have done in other places, listening to the stories and creating a piece of theatre.

As it turned out, Peterborough Archives (then part of the City Council) were about to apply to the Heritage Lottery Fund to do an oral-history project around the Peterborough Development Corporation (PDC) which had transformed the town, and to catalogue the two hundred boxes of archive material left behind by the PDC. However, the Archives were struggling to find means of public engagement, so we offered to do a play. I was also looking to do some oral history so we put the two projects together.

We started with stories of those who had moved there from London, and then we found we were able to speak to people who had worked for the Development Corporation. Peterborough has a long history, but most history books ended at 1968, saying 'and then the Development Corporation took over and that was that'. But we were now forty years on from that point, with two generations of people and families moving into the city and making it their own. So part of our pitch to the Heritage Lottery Fund was to create a play based on verbatim material from that period onwards.

*Parkway Dreams* was very much a mixture of the stories of those who moved to this 'new town', who were overspill from London and those who worked for the Development Corporation – they were able to tell us what worked and what went wrong.

*I'm interested to explore this idea of mixing 'verbatim' material and 'invented' play, how did you strike the balance with these two productions?*

To work with that kind of material you really have to make selections around specific issues and then give it to the actors to try out. I do believe this cannot be written and has to be done on the rehearsal-room floor. You can have the body of text and of course you need to make some selections of what to include, but there's no substitute for working with the actors and deciding what to keep and what to edit out. It's like a sculpture; you keep hacking bits off until you end up with the shape you want. Peter Cheeseman was right when he said it does have a sort of 'tang' to it, like salt in stew, that tells you this is authentic. Often something someone says comes out in an odd construction, which you shouldn't clean up too much, as no writer would ever write it like that and that's what gives it its magic.

However, I worry that this can go too far and I find the move toward 'mimicry' rather unsettling. I believe verbatim should be about *what* is being said rather than *how* it's being said. If you turn that round and put the emphasis on the *how*, then you corrupt it. By giving it to an actor it used to give the words of a working-class voice, often with a heavy regional accent, an authority – lifting up the working-class voices. Nowadays a lot of verbatim is about middle-class voices, which don't need that authority and so the emphasis has turned to the style and tone. Too much mimicry and we lose the content of what they are actually saying.

A lot of our work starts with the oral history and then the play is added on – putting the two together makes both stronger. There's nothing worse than fact-driven dialogue when you're focusing on a particular event, whatever it may be, and you are trying to shoehorn facts into a character's speech. Sometimes people accuse the writer of showing off their research, but often it's about helping the audience to understand the context, although too much can make it lumpy. By separating these two elements, the facts and the feelings, we can celebrate the content rather than apologising for it, allowing the audience to enjoy learning about how a fisherman goes about his work, for example, and then the play can concentrate on the characters.

*In* Parkway Dreams *you refer to characters by their title, rather than their name. Was this to avoid identifying high-profile figures such as Michael Heseltine?*

Well, we didn't give him a wig or anything like that, but it was clearly him and he was referred to by name in the play. Many of the others were referred to by their title, like 'The Housing Minister' or something, but that's because the ministers would change every year so we created one character that could amalgamate their comments. That said, where it was a recognisable figure, their personality would always come through: for example, Heseltine storming offstage in anger when someone disagreed with him – which is what he used to do in real life.

*And was that the same in* Beyond the Breakers?

For this I created completely invented characters – generalised lifeboatmen who represented the modern era, where they are no longer fishermen and have to go through modern health and safety procedures and training – who would celebrate their way of life. But yes, they were completed disguised. *Beyond the Breakers* was what I would call classic 'documentary theatre', as it took as its subject a specific craft, what I call 'hidden areas of experience', and revealed them to the audience. *Parkway Dreams*, however, was completely different, much more political so we were really finding our way with that one.

For *Breakers*, I took the actors to meet the lifeboatmen. We spent the day in Sheringham and went out on a trip. It's very important for the actors to meet the people whose stories we are trying to relate – they get the extra bits they need, the details, and they always come up with extra material. There is a strong element of trust; the actors need to trust the material, and the people they are portraying need to trust them.

○　○　○

## Alecky Blythe: Artistic Director, Recorded Delivery

Alecky Blythe began her theatre career as an actor, and, in 2003, she founded her company Recorded Delivery, creating her first verbatim-theatre piece, *Come Out Eli*. 'Recorded delivery' also refers to the very strict process in which Alecky approaches her verbatim material – all her interviews are recorded and played back to the actors through ear-pieces during rehearsals and the performance; then the actors repeat and copy what they hear rather than simply reading or learning the text. Since then, Alecky has risen to become one of the UK's most prominent practitioners of verbatim theatre. Her prominence is largely due to the groundbreaking verbatim musical *London Road* (which she wrote with composer Adam Cork) for the National Theatre in 2011. Prior to this, Alecky had already built up a significant body of work and, over a number of years creating verbatim plays on a range of subjects, she refined the specific methodology for which she is now renowned.

**The Girlfriend Experience** by Alecky Blythe
*Royal Court Theatre Upstairs (2008), and Young Vic (2009), both London*

For *The Girlfriend Experience*, Alecky spent time with sex workers in a brothel in Worthing, Sussex, gathering the real stories and experiences of those working in a profession surrounded by cliché and stereotypes. It is an exploration of the reality of those working in the industry, and an attempt to break through the misconceptions and the stigma of the 'oldest profession'.

In her review for the *Observer*, Susannah Clapp describes the production (directed by Joe Hill-Gibbins) and the effect of Alecky's techniques with verbatim material:

> Alecky Blythe's crackling verbatim drama offers different revelations: about the lives it puts on stage, and about the way you listen to dialogue. Blythe's method – brilliantly shown in *Come Out Eli* five years ago – is to record first-hand accounts and play the edited interviews, to the actors onstage through headphones: as they copy the hesitations, repetitions and gulps of ordinary speech, they expose the staid notions of normal talk.

Usually when people talk to themselves in a theatre, they're having a soliloquy: not here; they are muttering to keep going... These women aren't patronised or made into gargoyles: their sentences are gorgeous. They simply reveal their lives. What more could you want from the theatre?[6]

If we make a direct comparison with this technique and that of Ivan Cutting (and ACH Smith), we can see a stark contrast. Both Cutting and Smith allow room for invention to sit alongside verbatim, and would go further to suggest that each aspect is made richer by the presence of the other. Blythe's techniques, on the other hand, are much stricter and actively try to inhibit 'invention'. Her methodology is unapologetically concerned with presenting the interviewees' voices in the purest way possible, resisting the perhaps natural urge of actors and directors to overlay interpretation.

## In Discussion

### Alecky Blythe on Her Plays and Practice

*RB: Many people know you for the very specific techniques in approaching verbatim theatre; where did this process come from and how has it developed?*

AB: My process was based on that of Mark Wing-Davey [British actor and director], who in turn learnt it from Anna Deavere Smith [American actress and playwright]. To be specific, Mark taught that actors wear earphones in both rehearsals and performances, and copy exact speech patterns of the interviewees, and this is the process I used for my plays at first. For Anna's process, the earphones were only used in rehearsals and the actors learnt their lines for the performance. I did this for *London Road* and I'm using this method more and more; I suppose I'm going on a bit of a journey myself.

6. Susannah Clapp's review of *The Girlfriend Experience*, *Observer*, 5 October 2008.

With *London Road*, we worked with earphones in rehearsals for about six weeks and then the actors had to learn it. The recordings were still accessible, to refer to, but they had to learn them. I did go back to using earphones in performance for *Little Revolution* (at the Almeida), but they were actually a bit of a bind. The interviews were hard to hear, there was lots of background noise, so the actors ended up having to learn the lines anyway. The next show I'm doing will be without earphones in performance, but I will police it very tightly to make sure they don't miss an 'erm' or stop sounding like they do on the recording.

*How do you start creating a new piece of verbatim theatre?*

The starting point for me is often a news story, maybe something I've read in the newspaper or seen on the news. My plays are usually event-driven, so that is my way in. I then take myself off to those communities and record interviews, explaining that their words will become the script and actors will faithfully recreate their words onstage. I collect the audio and edit it down if I have time and that becomes the script. Or I may start with a subject and then I have to eke out a story.

*How do you go about 'eking out a story'?*

So with *Cruising*, which was my play about pensioners in search of passion, the central character was a lady called Maureen. Maureen had been a small part in another earlier show – *Strawberry Fields* – I had done a rough cut with Maureen as this small character and all the actors wanted to play her; but in the final draft I had to cut her as she was too far off-piste from the main narrative thrust. But after that show I went back to meet her, firstly to apologise that she had been cut but also to find out what she had been up to. She was a bit of a talker, really colourful, and she told me about her cruises and the forty-four men she'd been on dates with. She was on a quest to find the next love of her life and she was up for me chronicling that. She put me in touch with some of her dates, and with her friend Margaret who was also on the dating scene. I spent about nine months to a year on that one, digging around the subject.

With *The Girlfriend Experience*, I went to the Court saying: 'I want to make a play about prostitutes.' I had a contact who put me in touch with some high-class prostitutes and I thought I had an 'in', but they didn't lead me anywhere. They were too busy taking coke to be reliable interviewees. I then came across some blogs online and a woman who was running a parlour in Worthing. Once I got in touch with her I was able to talk to all the girls working there and find the stories: there was the new-business story, will it succeed or fail? And then these women were all trying to find love, so the other story was about whether it was possible to be in a relationship outside of their work.

It has to be a story you are interested in and for which you can find characters who will talk to you. The story has to push the play forward. The story's structure is crucial to make sure it's not just about anecdotes. You really have to put the time in, it's one of the downsides with verbatim work. I can't just block out some time and tell a theatre: 'I'm going to write this play.' I have to keep following the story or I might miss the story, that's the tricky thing with it.

*How do you work with your actors? Is it tricky to find actors who can adapt to the way you work?*

It's not for everyone and, yes, the audition process weeds out those who 'can' and those who 'can't' – I give them a crash course in working with earphones (even if they won't be used in performance). Not all actors like to be told how to say a line, which is what I have to do! They're thinking: 'where does this leave my craft?' But it requires all the same skills as if you were performing Mamet or Shakespeare, just in different ways. For those playwrights, the actor has to map the emotional journey, but with verbatim it's all mapped out already – that's what you've got to get to.

It can feel quite technical, quite dry, but it's still got to be 'connected', got to be 'sprung'. You have to make the audience feel like you're not doing it 'parrot fashion'. It takes enormous concentration and trust. It might seem gimmicky, all this, but actors have to learn to leave their egos at the door and trust that the way the interviewee said it, is the best way to say it. It may be difficult for actors to take that leap at first.

People often ask me: 'what sort of actors do I need?' – I need good ones! Actors who are open-minded to this way of working. Those who get it, love it, and they often tell me it informs the other work that they do, the more text-based work. They learn that, instead of always trying to 'do' something interesting with a line, sometimes people say the most profound things in the most mundane of ways.

Obviously verbatim work requires a lot of direct address. Actors get better at it the more they do, I don't often have time to teach them the game of tennis that happens between them and the audience. The audience is the interviewer, they're me, they're Alecky. So the actors are trying to relive the conversations I have had with the interviewees, trying to bring them to life. That's when it really works.

o    o    o

## Eking Out the Story

First let's return to our earlier question posed in Chapter One – **Why you? Why now?** What becomes extremely apparent when talking to both Ivan Cutting and Alecky Blythe, despite their differences of approach, is how important the story is to them. Both of them are responding to what they clearly see as a demand for the play, recognising that each of them was an important story and one that needed to be told. Whether one of these approaches feels like a more natural fit for you and your own work, or you are developing your own methods, there are useful lessons to be learnt from both these practitioners. If we now take a closer look at some of their key points, we will be able to unlock some simple principles for accessing the story within our own research and material.

# Devising and Improvisation

> To work with that kind of material you really have to make selections around specific issues and then give it to the actors to try out. I do believe this cannot be written and has to be done on the rehearsal-room floor.
>
> *Ivan Cutting*

It may feel counter-intuitive, as the very notions of 'devising' and 'improvisation' sit at the opposite end of the theatrical spectrum to verbatim, but as techniques to explore your material and subject they may prove useful. It may be that you will choose to take an approach like Ivan Cutting and interweave an invented narrative between the verbatim text, in which case this will assist in the creation of the 'invented' story and characters.

*HINT: Improvisation allows us to take a limited amount of knowledge (our parameters) and use our imagination to explore practically what lies in between. Therefore this process will be more appropriate for wider theme-based verbatim plays, where the material you have gathered is dominated by facts and figures rather than direct or individual experience.*

## Activity: Continuous Improvisation

○ *Ask yourself – what is the objective of this improvisation? What do we know and therefore what are we trying to learn?* With *Parkway Dreams*, for example, the Eastern Angles company began with masses of archive material that provided the background – historical, cultural and statistical evidence for what would have been the experience of a whole community or generation. This is a good example of when, with such a large 'collective' experience, it may be valuable to use this material to inform the parameters for exploring stories of an individual.

○ *Gather together key pieces of material that provide a 'backdrop' to your story* Try selecting the news items that examine the wider issue at hand, or descriptions of a key location. Perhaps you have only small extracts of text – brief quotes, social-media posts or soundbites that suggest an atmosphere or opinion, but lack detail.

○ *Provide your actors with the context*   Set some clear parameters from what you do know, so they can begin to explore the elements that are unknown. Ask them to create an imaginary character considering the following questions – some you will be able to answer immediately from your material, others you may have to propose an answer to begin with (you can always go back to explore other options later) and some may answer themselves through the playing of the improvisation.

### *Physical Context*

- Where are they? (Indoors? Outdoors?)
- What's their environment? (Weather? Temperature? Familiar or unfamiliar?)
- Who else is with them or are they alone?
- 'When' are they? (Year? Time of day? Season?)
- Are there any significant events that have taken place recently (or currently)?

### *Personal Context*

- Age?
- Gender?
- Cultural background? (Ethnic, regional, religious?)
- Personal background? (Key family and friends?)
- Do they hold significant opinions or attitudes?
- Physical clues (any information about their health or location which may have an effect on their physicality)?

○ *Set the 'objectives' and the 'opposition'*   We have touched on 'objectives' in Chapter Two, i.e. defining what a character wants to achieve in a particular situation. Also, it is often useful to identify what is working 'in opposition' to this desire – what is standing in their way?

○ *Play the improvisation*    I used the term 'continuous' earlier, which simply means to allow your actors to continue playing this scenario for as long as possible.

○ *Observe and record*    As director/writer, watching an improvisation on the outside, you want to observe the behaviour of different people under different circumstances – *these being always based upon the parameters set by your research.* What do you notice? Not everything will be of use, but does it provide any answers or raise more questions?

*HINT: It may be worth stressing that there is no need to invent 'drama'. Your subject, or context, will no doubt provide a dramatic context which is enough. If your actors begin to add or force more drama, your improvisation will soon veer into melodrama – if we were to identify a 'nemesis' for verbatim theatre, melodrama would be it.*

## Story vs. Statistics

The story has to push the play forward. The story's structure is crucial to make sure it's not just about anecdotes.

*Alecky Blythe*

If both practitioners mentioned in this chapter agree on one thing, it would seem to be the necessity of finding balance between the drive of the narrative and simply quoting fact. Blythe talks about making sure the play is 'not just about anecdotes', and Cutting similarly warns that 'there's nothing worse than fact-driven dialogue'. Even though 'anecdotes' and 'facts' are obviously not the same thing, the sentiment is the same.

Too many 'facts' are hard to for an audience to digest; it swiftly begins to feel more like a school lesson than a piece of theatre. This is especially the case when weaving in 'invented' dialogue; nothing will sound more false and unbelievable than a torrent of facts added to supposedly 'realistic' dialogue.

Equally, too many 'anecdotes' and the play will have nothing to drive it forward. We can imagine the plethora of stories Maureen and her friends had to share with Blythe, but without Blythe's sharp ability to edit and select the most appropriate stories, the play would feel rather more pedestrian, with no real focus.

### Activity: Building a Narrative

Test your story against these narrative principles.

○ *What happens*   Using all the information you have uncovered so far, have a go at putting the story down on paper, focusing on the key events or turning points. You may list it as a series of bullet points or it may be an interesting exercise, especially in a school environment, to write it out as a short story.

○ *Engaging vs. Informing*   Below I have listed two principles and offer them as elements that all good stories should contain.

  • *Engaging*   Which elements of the narrative appeal to an audience's sense of emotion or personal experiences? Will we sympathise with all/some of the characters on display? Will it entertain us? Will it horrify us?
  • *Informing*   Which elements of the narrative tell the audience the facts? Is it a presentation of the truth? Does it satisfy our curiousity? Does it reveal aspects of the subject that we might not have otherwise known?

○ *Does it balance?*   Taken as a whole, does the narrative strike a balance between being engaging and informing? Does one seem more prevalent than the other? Is one missing completely? Are you happy with the current balance or, if not, how can it be redressed?

*HINT: This is entirely subjective – it's your story and as leading practitioner you may decide that you are guided towards one principle over another. Don't forget that with verbatim theatre we are aiming to present truth, so you may need to check your own opinions aren't working in opposition to this.*

## Activity: Beginning, Middle and End

I'm certain everyone at school would have learnt that every good story has a clear beginning, middle and end. Looking at your bullet-point narrative structure, can you clearly identify these three phases? If your verbatim play is an event-based piece, then this activity will be fairly straightforward; if theme-based you may have to do a little more thinking.

*HINT: Identifying these three key moments in the story will give you an initial shape to the play and enable you to plan and ultimately edit your material to sustain the audience's attention. You may choose not to play scenes or events chronologically, so these refer to where they come in your play, and not necessarily in time/date order.*

### The Beginning

The event or discovery that kick-starts the story. It may be a disruption of the status quo, or many verbatim plays begin by outlining the issue that play is attempting to address.

Below is the opening page of *London Road* by Alecky Blythe and Adam Cork. There are several things worth noting here: first, the use of the audio recording instantly reminds the audience that what they are about to hear are real words from real people; secondly, it sets up the world of the play very clearly – it is the story of a neighbourhood, a community.

THE STORY

## ACT ONE

### Section One

*Church hall just off London Road.*

*The original audio recording of* RON'*s opening speech is heard over the PA in the auditorium. It fades out as* RON *starts to sing.*

### *Song – 'Neighbourhood Watch AGM'*

RON. *Good evening. (Beat.) Welcome. (Beat.) This really is our first AGM after we reconstituted in 2006 and then all the awful events happened and we became stronger an' stronger. Erm (Beat.) aft' so after our er reconstitution we made a lot – we made a lots of progress in regenerating this street. We've put new signs up, thanks to Ken. Hope-hopefully the problem with the girls has disappeared. We don't see them now. I believe there are still a few round in Hanford Road but er (Beat.) we really can't concern ourselves with them. The street has got much better in the last year. I think the police have done exceptionally well under exceptional circumstances to clear the streets as they have done. Our problem now is to keep them up so they may have commit them to Lo' – ya know – this is gonna continue. That they are still gonna help the girls who need helpin' or-or jump on the ones who don't. Our problem is to keep the police to that commitment. The Chief Constable said to us in the police briefing that this is gonna go on for five years. We gotta keep them to it! We can't let other priorities take – take over otherwise we're just gonna slip back. I wanna say 'thank you' to the police. Thank them becos representatives here and the Ward Councillors, the County Councillors who have done a lot to help us. An' so 'thank you very much all of you'. Yeah forthcoming events, Julie.*[7]

---

7. Alecky Blythe and Adam Cork, *London Road* (Nick Hern Books, 2011), p. 5.

It's a very inviting opening, suggestive of the main 'events', and yet it offers a reassuring glimpse of the end that the challenges are being overcome.

## The Middle

If you are going to have an interval, what is the event or question to end the first half – the 'cliffhanger' that will leave us in suspense and ensure we return for the second half? Or if it's a 'one-act' play, a carefully placed midway 'twist' or 'revelation' will keep the audience's focus.

Sticking with *London Road* as our example, Act One ends with the dramatic scenes outside Ipswich Magistrates' Court as the public and television crew await the arrival of Steven Wright – the man who was charged with murdering the sex workers. In this extract, the live commentary from BBC reporter Chris Eakin is heard simultaneously with the voices from the crowd.

> HINT: Note the use of repetition and overlapping voices, which increases the tension – and as the majority of this text is sung, the music too supports the play's climatic build toward the interval.

WOMAN 2 (*simultaneous*). *Hallo.*

MAN (*simultaneous*). *Hallo ARV.*

WOMAN 2. *Hallo. Hallo. They're closing in. (Pause.) They're closing in. (Pause.) They're obviously – he's obviously I comin' out cos they're closing in. They're closing in look. That's why all the police – I could see them stopping traffic an' that up there an' all.*

CHRIS EAKIN. Police motorbikes coming up the road – not from the direction we were expecting so I imagine this is not the convoy. (*Beat.*) Oh it **might** be actually. (*Beat.*) I think it is – these are the sirens from the right.

77

MAN. *Here he comes. 'Ere he comes.*

WOMAN 1. *Oh dear.*

WOMAN 2. *Yeah. Look at this. Look at this!*

WOMAN 1. *It's 'orrible innit eh? It's a wicked bloody world.*

*Beat.*

WOMAN 2 (*simultaneous*). *Hallo.*

MAN (*simultaneous*). *Hallo ARV.*

WOMAN 2. *Hallo. Hallo. They're closing in. (Pause.) They're closing in. (Pause.) They're obviously – he's obviously / comin' out cos they're closing in. They're closing in look. That's why all the police – I could see them stopping traffic an' that up there an' all.*

MAN. */ Here he comes. 'Ere he comes.*

WOMAN 1. *Oh dear.*

WOMAN 2. *Yeah. Look at this. Look at this!*

WOMAN 1. *It's 'orrible innit eh? It's a wicked bloody world. (Beat.) 'Ere they come.*

| | |
|---|---|
| *Loud sirens. The police van leaves the Court accompanied by a heavy police escort. The* CROWD *hurls abuse at the van... 'Get 'im outta here!', 'Scum!', etc.* | CHRIS EAKIN. It looks like we got Steven Wright now. (*Beat.*) An' here we have full convoy now. Steven Wright, forty-eight-year-old forklift-truck driver. |

*Crescendo builds of repeated final lines of chorus.*

*End of Act One.*[8]

---

8. Alecky Blythe and Adam Cork, *London Road* (Nick Hern Books, 2011), pp. 40–41.

## The End

What is this finale? Does it answer a question posed at the beginning? Maybe it brings the story full circle and ends where we began? Alternatively, could it end with the big 'event' that we were all waiting for? Or perhaps it ends with an unexpected twist?

With *London Road*, the end has echoes of the beginning and we see the proof the community's resilience. Following that opening speech, the character of JULIE (the London Road Neighbourhood Watch events organiser) describes how she had the idea of starting a 'London Road in Bloom' competition – the competition we see take place at the end of the play. In the extract below, the song 'London Road in Bloom' is a reprise, as this first occurs at the beginning of the play shortly after the speech from JULIE mentioned above.

> GORDON. *I'd just like to point out as well.*
> *It does seem that God is smiling on London Road.*
> *Cos if you'd seen the weather forecast for today.*
> *Well look at it now.*
>
> *Repeat x 9.*
>
> *Original audio recordings of various residents at the party are heard over the PA in the auditorium. They fade out as the music of the songs begins.*

### Song – 'London Road in Bloom' (reprise)

JULIE. *I got nearly seventeen hangin' baskets in this back garden – believe it or not. Begonias, petunias an' – erm – impatiens an' things.*

ALFIE. *Marigolds, petunias. We got up there, we got busy Lizzies, hangin' geraniums alright – / see the hangin' lobelias, petunias in the basket – hangin' basket. That's a fuchsia.*

DODGE. / *There's all sorts in that basket anyway.*

JAN. *Err there is a special name I just call them lilies. They're a lily type. There is a special name. An' for the first time this year I've got a couple of erm – baskets.*

TERRY. *Hangin' baskets, variegated ivy in there which makes a nice show. Then you've got err these sky-blue whatever they are ve – ver – ber la la. That's err little purple ones.*

HELEN. *Rhubarb, the old-fashioned margarites, the daisies.*

GORDON. *The roses have done really well this year.*

HELEN. *Gave an extra point for havin' basil on the windowsill didn't she. / Ha ha ha.*

GORDON. / *Yeah.*

*The End.*[9]

Here, at the end of Act Two, the repetition and overlapping of words (prompted in the text by the '/' symbol) is gentler and less threatening than the extract that ended Act One. What is a relatively ordinary, common community event has such poignancy in the knowledge of what they have overcome.

9. Alecky Blythe and Adam Cork, *London Road* (Nick Hern Books, 2011), pp. 78–9.

# 5. The Edit

*How to edit material successfully and sensitively and shape it into the story you want to tell*

To argue that one aspect of this process is more important than any other would be more than a little misleading; however, the editing stage is undeniably a crucial and delicate moment in the construction of any piece of verbatim theatre. It is at this point that you begin to sift and filter all the material you have collected; therefore it is the moment when your own voice is heard clearest as you select what will make the final draft, and what will be left on the cutting-room floor.

## Auditioning Material

One thing we know for certain is: **you simply cannot include everything**. By this stage you will have amassed a huge amount of material from a variety of sources, representing a range of voices and opinions. You need to begin to choose what will make the most beneficial contribution to your narrative.

### Activity: Assess Your Source Material

○ *Read and re-read your written sources*   Listen again to your interviews. As you do, make notes or highlight recurring themes or details.

○ *Check against your 'target board'*   Have you covered all the bases you intended to? Are there any gaps in your research or voices missing? Have you categorised them in the clearest and most appropriate way? Your original target board was created before the interviews were conducted, based on your initial judgements about what you *thought* people might offer; now you have spoken to them, this may have changed significantly.

○ *Explore the spectrum of voices*   With all material laid out in front of you, you will begin to see the spectrum of your material. Popular or commonly held views and experiences may already have become apparent to you during the interview stages; if not, they will begin to emerge now.

*HINT: As well as assessing what's there in front of you, it is important to look at what's not there. Is there a group or angle that is missing or unrepresented? If so, ask yourself what is the reason for this? Is it a gap in your research, or perhaps simply a minority opinion or a point of view no one is willing to express?*

Your role as a verbatim practitioner is to present a narrative using the original words used by experts, witnesses or those directly affected by the original event. It is your task and responsibility to decide what to do with these voices – which to lift up and which to suppress. Like the orchestration of a piece of music, a different mix of instruments will give the same piece of music a different sound; in the same way, different blends of voices will have distinctly different effects on your resulting script.

All the material that ends up in your piece should offer at least one of the following:

- ○ *Vital facts that place the piece in context for the audience.*

- ○ *A unique perspective* $\Big\}$ *not offered or expressed elsewhere.*
- ○ *An unrepresented voice*

If it doesn't offer any of these then it is a strong candidate for removal.

Of course, much depends on the subject and the story you have decided to tell with your piece, but many of these decisions will become evident as you gather your material and research.

---

**London Road** *by Alecky Blythe and Adam Cork*
*National Theatre, London (2011)*

In 2006 the bodies of five women were discovered in Ipswich. All the women were identified as sex workers who worked the same area of the town, around London Road. After a resident of the street was arrested, Alecky Blythe interviewed the other residents of the street to discover how they had been struggling, and come to terms, with these tragic events.

The majority of Blythe's interviewees were residents of the same road in Ipswich, and therefore it would be easy to categorise them all into one group and offer a general perspective from this group of people. However, Blythe and Cork are able to portray the different and detailed perspectives expressed by the individuals, who may in a different edit be portrayed as a single group with a shared experience and opinion. Blythe said:

> It would of course be a shocking experience for any community, but the fact that it took place in this otherwise peaceful rural town, never before associated with high levels of crime or soliciting, made it all the more upsetting for the people who lived there. It was not what was mainly being reported in the media about the victims or the possible suspects that drew me to Ipswich, but the ripples it created in the wider community in the lives of those on

the periphery. Events of this proportion take hold in all sorts of areas outside the lead story, and that is what I wanted to explore.[10]

# Revealing the Heart

During the process of interviewing, you may well have discovered that people often talk around the subject (especially if it is an emotional one) or thoughts are not expressed as eloquently as a playwright might compose them. Once you have decided that a particular voice or perspective is essential to your narrative, you may still have too much transcript material for inclusion. Before you take out the scissors or the red pen and begin to cut away, you must be sure you understand what lies at the heart of what's being said – or perhaps even not said!

Here are a few exercises I have found useful to help me and other practitioners reveal the heart of a transcript.

## Activities: Editing

### 1. Exploring the Text

In the same way an actor or director would do when looking at a certain scene of speech in a playtext, it's vital that you begin to get under the skin of your transcript. This process may be simpler if you have conducted the interviews yourself; however, these activities will enable you to gain a full understanding of your material.

> HINT: The following are text-based exercises, which is best done in the full knowledge of the clues found in the audio interview. As you proceed, make sure you remind yourself of the details and context in which the interview was conducted (as explored in Chapter Two). This information is crucial in order to maintain integrity in editing.

10. Alecky Blythe and Adam Cork, *London Road* (Nick Hern Books, 2011), Introduction, p. vii.

## a) ...for Meaning

○ *Read through the transcript*   Highlight all the sentences that offer information or explanation. These might be factual or mere opinion, they might be personal experiences or observed; either way, lift out the comments that provide the detail of actions or facts.

○ *Reduce the transcript*   Get it down to the bare bones of information on a separate page. Make a bullet-point list of each sentence or phrase.

○ *Examine the list closely*   How much of it is repeated information? Is it a series of eloquently explained facts (and/or opinions), or is it a catalogue of attempts to explain the same point over again? Or a mixture of the two?

*HINT: With this we are trying to uncover what they are really trying to say or express. It is essential to remember that your audience will make the final judgements. As editor, you have the ability to alter the meaning completely, but you also have a responsibility to remain sensitive and handle people's words and opinions with integrity. Identify what they say, not what you think they might be saying. We will take a closer look at the ethics of verbatim theatre in the next chapter.*

## b) ...for Emotion

○ *Go back to the original transcript and re-read*   This time, using a different colour, highlight all the sentences that offer clues to the interviewee's emotions or feelings. This could either be referring to events in the past (how they felt *then*) or at the time the interview was conducted (how they feel *now*).

○ *Revisit the notes*   You may also find it useful to look back at your transcript notes and any potential 'stage directions' (see page 38) that you made to accompany the interview. These will detail the non-verbal emotional indicators – pauses, sighs, crying, shouting and so on.

○ *Reduce*   As above, on a separate page, reduce the transcript to a bullet-point list of all the emotional references and indicators.

○ *Examine*   When you examine this list, it's important to remind yourself of the context of the interview – was it conducted in the midst of a major incident or was it an interview that looks back on events? Did the interview take place in formal surroundings (e.g. a press conference, or for a TV or radio interview), or was it more informal (e.g. the interviewee's home or workplace, or a neutral location)? The context may offer an insight into the emotional status of the interviewee.

*HINT: After exploring what they had to say, with this second activity we are trying to unpick and understand their* attitude(s) *towards it.*

Once you have mined the transcript for the information and emotional content you can begin to experiment with editing.

## 2. Editing for Time

First of all, it's always a good idea to ask yourself why you are editing this particular transcript. Would it be possible or even better to include in full? The main reason that most transcripts will need editing is time. You simply will not be able to use all the material you have gathered. Ultimately, you are constructing a play – you may already have time constraints related to the final performance but even if not, an acute sense of how long this story will be able to hold your audience's attention will be useful to you.

When leading workshops on creating verbatim theatre, I often use the following exercises that not only assist with what I call the distillation process (as I'm reminded of science experiments at school where we had to separate mixed liquid solutions into its purer parts), but also raise awareness of the power of the editor.

Below is the transcript of a speech taken from a project I led at the National Theatre Studio called *Hey U OK?* Working with young actors, we developed a verbatim play examining online dating and the role of social media within relationships. I will use this as source material, in order to illustrate the following activities.

JONATHAN (*a teacher*). Erm... The biggest thing for me is... obviously from an education point of view, erm, working with them... some of the time you want them to be able to leave the world outside, so you concentrate on what's needed. A... lot of young people today, have real problems about missing out on anything that's happening in their lives. Whereas... before the social-media stuff, you got... y... you... you'd wait till break-time, you'd catch up on... but now we have to get the phones off, turn them off, to be able to function. And... but the moment... erm, they go to their bags... phones are out and they're checking immediately. And... everything is instant. Now sometimes that can be a *good* thing... if you want... y'know... 's great... the immediacy of it. But when it comes to... sort of... the darker sides of... of... that social media... of privacy, sometimes there is no privacy and – (*Phone goes off and he reaches over to silence it, still talking.*) people's judgements... are... people's judgements are... erm... or people's opinions can go out... and it spreads like wildfire. (*Beat.*) The lies will spread. B... And once it goes onto Facebook, it's like... that's... that's it. It's gospel. It's the truth. And that's what's scary. (*Beat.*) So many students have used Facebook for... they say... 'We're in a relationship... it's now on Facebook.' And once it goes on Facebook, it's there... or the relationship is over... erm... and now it's official. It almost gives it... Facebook, this sense of sort of... law. But also there's this '*Frape*'? Where they get hold of each other's phones and therefore then put... messages and saying things, that *isn't* from them... but it goes out to everyone that it's from them. And actually, that can be, what seems as a *joke* can be really *dangerous*. So from my point of view it's just how it's used. Sometimes it's positive. But sometimes it's... too much importance is given to Facebook... and the sense of lack of actual communicating, *talking* – 'If it's on Facebook, we don't need to talk.' And it stops people communicating. You can go down and there'll be groups of students, *all* on their phones… but not talking to each other, not communicating with each other. But finding out about other people… and what they're doing… and commenting on what *they're* doing somewhere else. But not communicating amongst themselves… Erm… so yeah! Y'know. Yes it's great as a resource, to get messages out, but it just the quality of those messages and the importance of those messages.

### a) *The Five-sentence Edit*

Can you edit the original transcript down to the five key sentences or phases? Use your bullet-point lists to help you. Your five sentences *must* encapsulate the essence of the speech. The task is to distil the speech to reduce it down to what you know to be at its heart.

○ Here's my five-sentence edit of the above speech (yours may be completely different):

JONATHAN. Some of the time you want them to be able to leave the world outside, so you concentrate on what's needed.

A… lot of young people today, have real problems about missing out on anything that's happening in their lives.

But when it comes to… sort of… the darker sides of… of… that social media… of privacy sometimes there is no privacy.

Judgements or opinions can go out… and it spreads like wildfire.

Too much importance is given to Facebook… and the sense of lack of actual communicating, *talking* – 'If it's on Facebook, we don't need to talk.'

Can you distil the speech even further and reduce it to two sentences or phrases?

○ My two-sentence edit:

> JONATHAN. A… lot of young people today, have real problems about missing out on anything that's happening in their lives.
>
> Too much importance is given to Facebook… and the sense of lack of actual communicating, *talking* – 'If it's on Facebook, we don't need to talk.'

## b) *The Ten-word Edit*

Go that stage further and identify the ten words that still give the fullest sense of the whole speech, in terms of informative as well as emotional qualities. These ten words don't need to add up to a complete sentence, the idea is not to construct a phrase that's not there, instead they should simply be a collection of single words (or short phrases) that provide a raw sense of what was expressed in the full transcript.

○ My ten-word edit:
  - *Social media.*
  - *Judgements.*
  - *Like wildfire.*
  - *Dangerous.*
  - *Lack of communicating, talking.*

Can you go to five words? One word even?

○ My five-word edit:
  - *Facebook.*
  - *Judgements.*
  - *Like wildfire.*
  - *Dangerous.*

○ My one word:
  - *Dangerous.*

  *HINT: You'll no doubt have noticed that the less you include, the more subjective you have become. The one word I chose as the most important was 'dangerous' – that to me seemed to be at the heart of what he was trying to tell me about the subject. However, if I asked Jonathan to choose himself, he may well have chosen differently! Think of that school science experiment, you've separated the solution, but you must decide which of the parts to keep and which to discard.*

## 3. Editing for Meaning

This exercise is especially useful if you are working on a speech from someone with strong opinions; a politician, for example. The challenge is to re-edit the text to alter meaning completely. See my example below where I re-edit this teacher's speech to appear he is arguing the exact opposite to his original transcript. The number one rule is: you must *not* add any words, just make cuts and play with what's there.

○ My 'inside out' edit. First I have highlighted the phrases I will use...

JONATHAN. ~~Erm… The biggest thing for me is… obviously from an education point of view, erm, working with them… some of the time you want them to be able to leave the world outside, so you concentrate on what's needed. A… lot of young people today, have real problems about missing out on anything that's happening in their lives. Whereas…~~ *before the social-media stuff, you got… y… you… you'd wait till break-time,* ~~you'd catch up on…~~ *but now* ~~we have to get the phones off, turn them off, to be able to function. And… but the moment… erm, they go to their bags… phones are out and they're checking immediately. And…~~ *everything is instant.* ~~Now sometimes~~ *that can be a* good *thing…* ~~if you want…~~ *y'know… 's great… the immediacy of it.* ~~But when it comes to… sort of… the darker sides of… of… that social media… of privacy, sometimes there is no privacy and – (Phone goes off and he reaches over to silence it, still talking.) people's judgements… are… people's judgements are… erm… or people's opinions can~~

~~go out... and it spreads like wildfire.~~ (*Beat.*) ~~The lies will spread. B... And once it goes onto Facebook, it's like... that's... that's it. It's gospel. It's the truth. And that's what's scary. (Beat.) So many students have used Facebook for... they say... 'We're in a relationship... it's now on Facebook.' And once it goes on Facebook, it's there... or the relationship is over... erm... and now it's official. It almost gives it... Facebook, this sense of sort of... law. But also there's this~~ *'Frape'?* ~~Where they get hold of each other's phones and therefore then put... messages and saying things, that isn't from them... but it goes out to everyone that it's from them. And actually, that can be, what seems as~~ *a joke* ~~can be really dangerous.~~ *So from my point of view it's just* ~~how it's used. Sometimes~~ *it's positive. But sometimes it's... too much importance is given to* ~~Facebook... and the sense of lack of actual communicating, talking~~ *'If it's on Facebook, we don't need to talk'. And it stops people communicating.* *You can go down and there'll be groups of students, all on their phones...* ~~but not talking to each other, not~~ *communicating with each other.* ~~But~~ *finding out about other people... and what they're doing...* ~~and commenting on what they're doing somewhere else. But not communicating amongst themselves...~~ *Erm... so yeah! Y'know. Yes it's great as a resource, to get messages out,* ~~but it just the quality of those messages and the importance of those messages.~~

...and here's how I stitched it back together again...

JONATHAN. Before the social media-stuff, you got... y... you... you'd wait till break-time, but now everything is instant. That can be a *good* thing... y'know... 's great... the immediacy of it. Sometimes too much importance is given to *'Frape'.* From my point of view it's positive, a joke. You can go down and there'll be groups of students, all on their phones… communicating with each other. Finding out about other people… and what they're doing… Erm… so yeah! Y'know. Yes it's great as a resource, to get messages out.

It's rough and it's crude, but by doing this exercise with young actors or students (or even for yourself), it simply demonstrates how easy it is to edit someone's words to shift their original meaning completely – and yet in the broadest sense the above could still be classed as 'verbatim'; it is after all their own words!

> HINT: The most important rule in setting this up as an exercise is the participants must not add anything, but only edit and shuffle the words given by the interviewee.

We are probably most familiar with the power and effects of editing with regards to filmmaking and perhaps even more familiar with television. The current mass of reality-TV programmes rely heavily on an entertaining edit. Nothing is added – everything that's shown took place in (some sort of) reality; however, the order in which things were said may have been altered and, crucially, what was lost in the footage that never made the final cut? Well-meaning sentiments taken out of context can give unintended meaning – it is the age-old attack on journalists from those who feel they have not been well represented in the print media too, that their comments were 'taken out of context'. Or perhaps showing an explosive display of emotion, but not showing the full events that led up to that explosion; therefore the person appears to the audience as irrational or unreasonably aggressive.

> HINT: The reason to include this activity is to demonstrate how easy it is to misrepresent the interviewee, even though you may have the best intentions. I refer to this as the 'Frankenstein edit' – our intentions were good, to recreate the voice and opinions of the original, but we have inadvertently created a monster!

So when you are editing your interviews, ask yourselves why you have to edit at all: for **time**, to get to the heart of the story quicker? Or for **meaning**, to make the heart clearer?

# Structure and Narrative

Having worked on editing your source material, you will really start to understand what is at the core of those statements and testimonies. By this time too you should have a clear idea of the narrative that has emerged from your research – how your story is being told through these words? Now you need to consider very carefully the best way of telling that narrative. Thoughts and ideas about how you structure your verbatim piece will probably be emerging and, in my experience, they keep changing and shifting as the process moves along.

Here are a few points to consider as you begin to shape your story; some may be more pertinent than others, depending on the subject of your verbatim play.

## *Slow release of information*

One of the skills of playwriting in general is the ability to carefully time the release of information to the audience. You want their interest to develop and last the whole play and so you must avoid revealing too much too soon.

## *A mix of voices*

Audiences find it quite hard to listen to the same voice for a long period of time, the danger being your piece ends up feeling more like a lecture than a play. Find interesting ways of mixing up interviews, e.g. intercutting between two interviews or splitting up one long interview into smaller sections throughout the play.

## *Balance of opposing opinions*

Following on from point 2, you can find some very interesting ways of balancing different perspectives. You might decide to put those offering similar voices together so your audience receives one argument in full, followed by an opposing one. Alternatively you can find more creative ways of splicing the two together and create a unique virtual discussion between two or more parties.

## Chronology

If your play deals with a particular event, you may find it useful to keep interviews that talk specifically about what happened in chronological order. However, playing with time can offer some very interesting results (see the following case study), but be careful it doesn't jeopardise clarity and understanding for your audience.

## Thematic links/parallels

With the activities outlined in previous chapters, you may have already made thematic links between transcripts. One way of structuring your play is quite simply to present these together in sections, like a play is divided into scenes.

## Balance of tone

This is especially important to bear in mind if you are tackling a difficult or potentially upsetting subject or event. Although graphic and hard-hitting accounts provide drama and poignancy, an hour or more of non-stop distress and suffering may feel relentless, and your audience's interest may begin to wane. Find a balance of facts and speculation, comic and tragic; this will both keep your audiences engaged and also enable the serious moments to really stand out and have a powerful effect.

## Length

A key factor in all your editing is having a strong idea of the desired length of your piece. Will it be one act or two? The amount of material you have collected will dictate this to some extent. But is there a natural halfway point, a twist in the story, a game-changer that would serve as a suitable moment for an interval? Equally (and especially if your subject is particularly hard-hitting), it may be wise to keep it short and punchy.

## Dramatic tension

Like any good story, your piece needs to keep the audience engaged throughout, carefully leading them through the twists and turns. If you are dealing with a specific event, it will naturally build towards a climax (or maybe several), so make sure that your edit enhances and supports that natural momentum. With a theme-based play, you may have to work a little harder and deliberately structure material in order to keep up the pace and tension.

## Your audience

All the notes listed above can only really be tackled if you have a clear idea of who your audience will be. Knowing that your play is going to be performed in a school assembly will lead to different editing choices from those made for a production at the Edinburgh Festival Fringe, for example. If your play deals with issues in a particular community, will members of that community also be your audience? If so, you will need to think carefully about whether you are celebrating or criticising them.

*Walking the Chains* by ACH Smith
*Walking the Chains CIC, in association with Show of
Strength Theatre and Circomedia (2015)*

ACH Smith had previously written the highly successful verbatim play *Up the Feeder, Down the 'Mouth* using testimony from those who worked on the Bristol Docks up until they closed down in 1973. He was then asked to create another piece as a celebration of the 150th anniversary of Clifton Suspension Bridge. His play took the historical story of how the bridge was built and combined it with the verbatim stories and experiences of those who work on the bridge today. He interviewed the bridgemaster, maintence crew, toll-booth keepers and tour guides, as well as members of the public – Bristolians who had stories to share about this landmark, which is a symbol of the city.

I was approached to direct this play and, for about a year, worked closely with Smith as his dramaturg. The two main challenges in the editing process were, firstly, finding an appropriate balance of 'tone' and, secondly, the balance of history and contemporary material.

With regards to the tone of the play, much of the material Smith had collected was heavily based on fact and often incredibly detailed. A crucial factor, not to be ignored, was that the building of the bridge was in itself a remarkable feat of science and engineering. However, the play was not intended to be merely a 'science lesson', and so bold decisions in the editing process were needed in order to remove 'facts' that weren't essential to telling the story or illustrating the engineering achievement.

Early drafts of the play told the story in a strict chronological order – Act One told the story of Isambard Kingdom Brunel and the building of the bridge, and Act Two dealt almost exclusively with the contemporary material. The final draft that was presented ended up mixing both halves together, and so the play took you back and forth between the nineteenth century and the modern day. The chronology of the bridge's construction was all played in the correct order, only the modern text was injected into the story at appropriate moments. The decision to do this became of significant value, providing part of the solution to the challenges of 'tone'; a montage of voices was created offering a wide spectrum of different eras, backgrounds and perspectives, and rather than 'scenes' the play had numbered sections containing material that was thematically linked.

This was a piece of theatre designed to celebrate an icon of the city, and that had a significant impact on our decision-making. Presenting this play with its strong local ties had huge advantages, such as the audience's knowledge of key people, places and the bridge itself. However, that also carries a significant amount of pressure to be accurate – facts, details, accents and so on were all under the fiercest of scrutiny.

The following extract from ACH Smith's *Walking the Chains* serves as a good example of the way the production moves between different time periods. This was a decision I made in my role as dramaturg. I took the strands of the historical story that Smith had written and placed them next to sections of verbatim material from the modern-day interviews. I felt it was important that the different extracts would connect and so, on occasion, I would ask Smith to re-edit the verbatim or redraft the historical 'play' in order that the two strands would interplay and speak to each other. In the section below, we dealt with the sensitive subject of suicides – both of us were keen that this section remained in the play, despite an initial nervous hesitation from the Clifton Suspension Bridge Trustees. Like it or not, the Clifton Bridge was (and still is) a popular suicide site and both Smith and I did not want the production to shy away from the difficult issues.

As a director, I was keen to explore this interplay between the historical and the modern, in a way that meant all actors were sharing the same space, and aware of each other. Both sides of this particular coin were contributing, simultaneously to the story of the Clifton Bridge. The story of Sarah Henley is famous in Bristol – the girl who threw herself off the bridge only to be saved by her own dress. Here Smith took the information he discovered about her and wrote a scene that is essentially fiction, an imagining of what might have happened, based on the facts he could source; although the last section was edited from an original recording of an interview she gave for the BBC. The characters of Lucy, John, Dan and Neil are from the modern day and based on real people (although the names and identities have been changed).

Lucy is a tour guide. This being such a famous story in the life of the Clifton Bridge, it was one that featured in every tour-guide's repertoire.

John, Dan and Neil are the bridge-maintenance crew, and although they were characterised by the dry Bristol sense of humour, this aspect of the job still affected them all very deeply.

All the other named characters are part of the 1885 (non-verbatim) account of Sarah Henley's story.

**Scene 6**

SARAH. People will tell you that...

LUCY. Sarah Henley...

SARAH....that's me, Sarah Henley, was a sweet girl heartlessly crossed in love who in 1885 jumped from the bridge but landed gently on the mud because my crinoline acted as a parachute.

JOE (*to* ENSEMBLE). Oh yeah? To start with, she's twenty-two years of age, no girl any more. And she will never leave off giving I grief, no matter what I does or says, till I've just about had my fill on it, and I thinks, I can't spend the rest of my life like this. So I writes her a letter to tell her so, trying to put it nicely, like.

SARAH *storms forward toward* JOE, *she is accompanied by her* FATHER.

FATHER. C'mon, my girl, tell him.

SARAH (*to* JOE). You needn't think I can't do better for myself than marry a railway porter, oh no, I've got gentlemen courting me.

JOE (*laughing*). Good on yer, girl, you go off now and ride to your wedding in a fine carriage!

SARAH *storms off.*

JOHN. I'm in my booth as normal, keeping an eye on the bridge…

FATHER *squares up to* JOE *and lands him one on the nose and exits.*

JOE. Well, I thinks that was the end of it, draw a line under. (*Exits.*)

JOHN.…when I see a young lady climb over the railings, perch on the parapet… and before I can get to her, she jumps off. (*An* AERIALIST *descends.*) The wind is blowing up, south-west as usual. It takes her skirts, bringing her over towards the Clifton side. Then she turns a complete somersault. What saves her life is that she ends up falling with her feet pointing downwards, so that the air catches under her skirts. Still, she hits on the mud there with a fearful smack.

LUCY. Two men who had witnessed her fall wade into the mud and bring her to the bank of the river. The police are summoned, and a doctor from Hotwells, who advises that she needs to be taken at once to the Bristol Infirmary. The policeman sends for a cab to come from the cab-stand on Dowry Square.

CABMAN. I'm not having that in my cab.

COPPER. She is in urgent need of surgical attention.

CABMAN. I'm sorry to hear that, but look at the state of her. I've just had my cab in for cleaning and repair. All that mud on her, that would mean another day I'd be without work.

DOCTOR. Have you no heart? She is near the point of death.

CABMAN. Double fare, and a ten-pound deposit on my cleaning bill.

DOCTOR. Fetch that wheelbarrow over here.

COPPER. Sir. (*He does.*)

DOCTOR. And I hope they keep a special cab rank in hell for you.

CABMAN. It's all very well you cursing me, but you don't understand.

LUCY. It was an hour before they got Sarah to the Infirmary.

SARAH. During the weeks I spent in there, recovering from shock and internal injuries, my fame spread abroad. I received offers of marriage from gentlemen, and invitations from showmen to tour the country. Eventually, I married Mr Lane, of Easton, had children and grandchildren, and lived to the age of eighty-four. A year before I died, in 1948, the BBC got me to talk into their microphone.

*Song – 'Crossed in Love'*

JOHN. It's human nature to try and stop someone from killing themselves. It's the ones who just say 'good morning' and go on, we can't do nothing about them.

DAN. When you talk to them, sometimes they are aggressive, sometimes they are submissive. I've had people in my face saying: 'just let me go.' There's no training for that.

JOHN. The coastguard brings the boats out. That's the sad bit of the job really.

NEIL. The scary thing is, they can be talking to you and you've built up a relationship, haven't you? Over a fifteen-minute period, you have built up a picture of that guy and he knows what I am about, but he doesn't want your help, he wants to end his life, and that picture sticks in your head and that never goes. The only thing I would like to see is some feedback when you've talked them back. What happened to that guy?[11]

Hopefully this chapter, and the examples and activities it offers, will help you understand what lies at the heart of your material, and how you can begin to shape your play by making editorial decisions that will tell your story and preserve the integrity of the interviewees.

As I was with *Walking the Chains*, you can be really creative and explore the different ways to present this; sharing your chosen story in a way that honours the material and that challenges, provokes and entertains your audience.

THE EDIT

11. ACH Smith, *Walking the Chains* (unpublished, 2014).

# 6. The Ethics

*How to remain responsible as a practitioner while being creative with other people's words*

The word 'ethics' is related to the ancient Greek word 'ethos' meaning 'customs' or 'habits'. I would always advocate that any verbatim-theatre practitioner should conduct themselves in an ethical way, and therefore our habits, our customs, our very practices must in themselves be ethical. By this I mean they are carried out with honesty and integrity.

I say here 'must', rather than 'should', because the pursuit of the verbatim play is to reveal truths (as far as we are able), not to deal in gossip, rumour or hearsay. That said, in our modern world it is very hard to define many moral or ethical absolutes – any definitive **dos** and **don'ts** – and therefore we find ourselves in the undeniably grey area, relying more on our own sense of what we **should** or **should not** do.

I am not qualified as a legal expert or moral philosopher, nor am I required to be. However, I do require – in fact, I demand – that my conduct and creative pursuits are led by respect, honesty and integrity. If these are our only **must-dos**, we can't go far wrong with our assumptive **shoulds** and **should-nots**. Without the security of many absolutes, this book, and especially this chapter, can never be considered a rulebook, but simply a guide.

## Rights and Responsibilities

Thanks to the UN's Universal Declaration of Human Rights, you, of course, have the 'right to freedom of opinion and expression'. The specific section of the treaty that articulates this, reads as follows:

**Article 19**

Everyone has the right to freedom of opinion and expression; this right includes freedom to hold opinions without interference and to seek, receive and impart information and ideas through any media and regardless of frontiers...[12]

So as an artist you have the right to express your opinions through your work. But how far do you have the right to manipulate or restrict the same rights of other people? Even Amnesty International, an organisation that has gained huge respect across the world for its tireless campaigning for Human Rights, acknowledges that free speech does occasionally have legitimate restrictions and more importantly is clear that as a **right** it requires a **responsibility**.[13]

Let's be honest, the very process of 'editing' is in some way to restrict someone's voice, but there is a line between **editing** and **censorship**. With a fictitious play, the line is clear, the audience enters the theatre knowing full well that what they are about to see and hear are the opinions and attitudes of the characters which have derived from the creative mind of the writer(s) and may (or may not) reflect their own view of the world. You often will see the disclaimer on films and television programme that the characters in the drama are not 'based on real people', or 'any similarity is coincidental', or words to that effect. Political writers have for centuries been treading this line

12. Taken from the United Nations website; you can read all thirty articles of the Declaration at www.un.org/en/universal-declaration-human-rights.
13. For further reading visit: www.amnesty.org.uk/free-speech-freedom-expression-human-rights.

very carefully. Commentary on Shakespeare's plays, for example, is continually drawing parallels with the political climate of the Elizabethan and early Jacobean period; however, to cross the line and openly criticise the monarch or their government back in the sixteenth century meant prison or worse (as many of Shakespeare's contemporaries found out the hard way).

That line becomes somewhat blurred when, as we do with verbatim, we openly use the words of other people. By declaring that 'they said it' we are feeding it to the audience as a 'truth' that cannot be contested – after all, it's not our words but theirs: 'they said it'! Actor Peter Temple gives a good example of this (see Chapter Seven) when he described how a women took offence to the portrayal of local people in a particular verbatim production. The company's recourse, in effect, was: 'we're just repeating what *they* said, you can't argue with it.' This is true, with perhaps one minor exception – those recordings were all edited. Extracts of the original audio were removed and at some point decisions were taken as to what needed to be included and what would be taken out. Why wouldn't they? As we have already discussed, if you left everything in, the play would go on for hours and hours, with much of it being irrelevant or, worse yet, boring! Whatever the reason, we cannot forget that although on the whole the text may be verbatim, it has still been through a process – and a subjective, judgemental process at that. The audience don't have this power, they can only hear what is being told to them; that power belongs to, and is the responsibility of, the practitioner – you. The audience's power is different, they can choose to believe or not, but like with documentary films or news items, when something is presented as truth, an audience will more often than not receive it as such.

It's at this point where the Greek word 'ethos' displays its second meaning. Ethos was considered one of the three branches of rhetoric – the art of persuasive speech – the other two being pathos (emotion) and logos (logic). As well as a sense of moral argument, the use of 'ethos' in classical rhetoric was to assert one's authority on the chosen subject. For example: the doctor talking about the NHS, the teacher discussing the education system or the lollipop man/lady on road safety. You will be seeking such authorities to interview on your chosen subject and will ultimately present yourself (albeit by proxy via their authority) as an authority on the whole subject – someone who knows the whole story, knows more than most, knows the 'truth'. The television producers present themselves as the authority when they air reality-TV shows like *Big Brother*; they are the ones who have seen all the footage, so, we assume, they are best placed to edit it down enough so we can get the story of the day in an hour-long show. As an audience, we automatically accept their authority and instinctively trust their integrity; we only have reason to doubt and question when we receive contrary information (either through their own bad editing, or from another source).

Sticking with the television theme, we are all familiar with the clichéd courtroom-drama oath (based on real court proceedings), whereby a witness swears that they will 'tell the truth, the whole truth and nothing but the truth'. Can we, as verbatim practitioners, hold ourselves up to this oath, willing (if only in a hypothetical court) to testify in the defence of our art? As they stand, the first and last would seem pretty straightforward:

To tell **the truth** is what verbatim theatre sets out to achieve; by its very nature it offers the audience a greater sense of truth, opening up an event or issue for close examination.

To tell **nothing but the truth** would therefore follow on naturally. Verbatim theatre does not knowingly offer falsehoods or propagate myths, because the text is the real words spoken by 'experts' – those who have superior knowledge of the subject/event, experienced it, were witness to it or directly affected by it.

Our sticking point comes with the middle section – **the whole truth**. We have already established that it is inevitable that we must cut something. But does cutting anything put us immediately in breach of this principle? Not necessarily; the deletion of a few lines where an interviewee went off-topic would not deny the audience any of the 'whole truth'. It may deny them a little added insight into the life, attitude or thought process of that individual, but, depending on your project, that may not be of use or interest. In our editing though, we must ensure that we remain faithful to the full argument or opinion that any individual or group offers us. That offering is a gift, whether we agree with it or not, and we must treat it as such. I refer back to the Declaration of Human Rights – our subjects are also entitled to that right and their rights must be treated with the same respect as our own. The exercises offered in Chapter Five are designed to heighten our awareness of the whole truth, and sharpen the skills needed to simply reduce the word count and not the content or the sentiment.

## Activity: Responsibilities of Practitioners

So what are your responsibilities as a verbatim practitioner? Are you able to define them?

○ *Discuss in groups*   In small groups (or as individuals) can you complete the sentence:

> *As verbatim practitioners, our responsibility is to...*

You may have several answers or 'responsibilities'.

○ *Make notes*   On small separate bits of paper or sticky notes, write each 'responsibility'.

○ *Lay it out*   When you have finished, lay out all the pieces of paper on the floor and group similar phrases together.

○ *Agree?*   Do we all agree or are there some answers which cause disagreement?

○ *Reach a consensus*   From here, are you able to come up with a complete list on which the whole company can agree?

*HINT: How companies operate and conduct themselves will vary and depend largely on your topic, but it's a good idea to make sure that everyone is working towards the same aim and governed by similar principles.*

○ If you are leading a group in which different subjects will be interviewed by different people, it can be worth extending your list of responsibilities to clarify a set of principles. It can be as formal or informal as you feel appropriate, but these principles may give you the peace of mind that interviews and research will be collected with integrity by your company members.

In your discussions, depending on your subject, you may find examples where you feel some people are not deserving of your respect, and therefore you do not feel the same sense of responsibility. I'm thinking of perhaps the criminal who has committed a terrible crime or the politician whose decision caused widespread harm or devastation. It's easy to cast the villain, the figure that allows us to rally together and feel secure in our hatred, and in some cases that will be what you choose to do; but however tempting it may seem, trial-by-verbatim theatre is to reduce your piece to little more than cultural vigilantism. Even the tribunal plays don't offer a 'verdict', but offer the verbatim testimonials so the audience can come to their own conclusions. Likewise, a play like *London Road* could have easily become a 'whodunnit', but instead was far more concerned in offering an insight into a community that felt (and continues to feel) the effects of the events depicted. As a result the audience gained a deeper, richer understanding of those events, through the voices of people they wouldn't have otherwise heard from.

Below is some terminology you might find useful when discussing these issues. It's at this point where I remind you, **these are not legal definitions** – you are responsible for seeking the appropriate legal advice if you have any concerns relating to your topic. These are merely to introduce a few pitfalls to avoid as guidance towards what we might define as 'best practice'.

## Slander

Oral untruths: making false (spoken) statements about someone, which may tarnish their character. As such, slanderous statements or comments may be grounds for the subject to seek legal action in order to defend their reputation. It goes without saying that your production and company won't want to fall foul of the law, so facts must be checked and opinions clearly offered as such.

## Libel

Written untruths: as with slander, except the false statement is published in print. In your marketing and publicity material (flyers, posters, websites, etc.) you will want attention-grabbing copy, and many companies may want to court controversy when tackling thorny topics but, as above, make sure you are not inadvertently breaking the law.

## Plagiarism

Copying someone else's work and claiming it as your own. Work that already exists may be subject to copyright laws. You will need to seek permission for all images, photography and music that you use in your performance or marketing, and may need to credit the original artists. This not only applies to written or published work; ideas too may be considered 'intellectual property'.

## Undercover recording

In most circumstances, as outlined in Chapter Two, you would obtain permission to make an audio or video recording of the interview. However, you may feel there are suitable justifications to record in secret as you may not get an accurate or honest response if the subject is aware of the filming. Although many journalists rely on undercover recording, and we see the results of such 'sting' operations regularly in the press, this does lead us into another distinctly grey area. In their 'Editorial Guidelines' the BBC outline a sound approach to this area, stating:

> Secret recording will normally involve an infringement of privacy and, when it does, we must therefore ensure it is editorially justified. Our actions should be proportionate to

the public interest they serve: the greater the infringement of privacy, the higher the public interest required to editorially justify it.[14]

The site goes on to outline in detail the BBC's policy and various differing circumstances, which is useful reading – and while it may seem overwhelming (it is designed for a large corporation), it contains sound principles of justification and decision-making.

○   ○   ○

Time and time again, the verbatim practitioner is required to call into question their decisions and their decision-making process. Many verbatim plays are born out of a sense of moral injustice – a need to right a wrong, set the story straight or give a voice to the voiceless. But whatever the subject and the story, in order to navigate through the grey mists of ethics, we need to ensure that our agenda is in check and continue to ask ourselves: '**are my choices being made in the best interest of telling the story in the clearest, most engaging way possible; whilst at the same time retaining integrity towards its subject?**'

14. www.bbc.co.uk/editorialguidelines/guidance/secret-recording/guidance-full.

# 7. The Actors

*How to support the actors' process, and what form that process might take*

A story is only as good as its teller. Similarly, a piece of theatre is only as good as the actors who perform it. Of course, you need a good script, but that's not enough; theatre relies on the live interaction between performers and audience, and this relationship is particularly delicate when it comes to verbatim theatre. In this chapter we will cover some practical activities and principles to help you, as a director, get the best from your acting company.

We will also gain an insight from three actors who have all had experience of rehearsing and performing in verbatim plays. Although each production was created using a different process, it's interesting to note the similar challenges they had to overcome, as well as those unique to each production.

# In Discussion

## Paul Thornley

*Paul Thornley trained at the Guildford School of Acting. He was in the original cast of* London Road, *and spoke to me about being launched in at the deep end with his first experience of performing verbatim theatre.*

RB: *So you were in the original cast of* London Road *at the National; how did you find that experience, working within Alecky Blythe's process? You've performed in other musicals before, but I imagine this was quite different.*

PT: Well, I think she had to rewrite her own rulebook when it came to *London Road*, because it was a musical. Her usual method of using the earpieces and following a couple of seconds behind just wasn't practical, because you couldn't hear the thing that was going on in your ear, plus the fact you were trying to listen to the music.

*So you did actually try having the earpieces in rehearsals at the beginning?*

Yeah, and we got ourselves into a terrible state in rehearsals and gave up on that very quickly. But we constantly listened. I'd never had any experience of verbatim theatre before this came up but, y'know, when you get an audition at the National for something new and exciting you just go: 'yep, we'll give that a go.' I then had the experience of listening to a recording and working two seconds behind and it's a very odd experience. I think sometimes you go to an audition and you think: 'I've got to show them what a terrific actor I am', but you haven't got time for that, because you're so busy listening to all the 'ums' and tics and 'ahs' and trying to get it exactly. That's what Alecky requires and she believes, quite rightly, that the accuracy is what makes it so compelling. Being as exact as that, something happens and it works; if people are paraphrasing in any way at all, it doesn't.

The liberating thing about doing it with the listening is that you're simply a vessel, a mouthpiece for their voice. You have to put your ego out the way. If you want to become an actor and start breaking down in the middle of the stage, bursting into tears and pouring your heart out, that doesn't really happen – in my experience – in verbatim theatre.

Because actually people talk about tragedy and comedy in very much the same passive way and that's what's fascinating about it. We were talking about some rather grisly murders and you listen to the tape and someone will break off in mid-sentence and start talking about taking jacket potatoes out the oven. It's the 'ordinariness' of normal speech which is so fascinating. I learnt an awful lot from that and the fact that people can talk about terrible things in a very, very calm way.

So what we had to do was, we all had to work out our own notation, by learning one line of dialogue at a time, listening to it over and over and over again. I mean, it can take two or three hours just to get one line. Alecky was very strict about it, quite rightly. So we all drove ourselves absolutely mad, listening to these people over and over and over again.

I hadn't seen a picture of my character, nor did I want to see a picture of him because the physicality just comes from the listening, I think. Suddenly you find you're playing this person who isn't you and the more you can let that happen, the better, rather than trying to force something on it – that was my experience – and that's where the naturalness of it comes.

*It's interesting that you say you didn't want to see a picture of your character; I know Alecky did an enormous amount of research and there were recordings that weren't used. Did you have to do any extra research on top of what Alecky brought to the process?*

Not really; she gave us a brief description of who these people were, but never a physical description, she tried to let us do that. There was a massive amount of material. When we started doing *London Road*, we didn't know what was going to be used and what wasn't, so I did listen to lots of things that didn't end up in the play, which was really useful just to hear his speech patterns – he had a slightly rolly 'r' which came and went.

In terms of accents, the dialect coach from the National came and said things like 'in Ipswich they use this vowel', but the reality is, people change. Your fear as an actor is: 'if we say it like he does on the tape everyone will think we're not consistent', but people aren't consistent, it depends on who they're talking to and what time of day. In the same way that people when they talk to taxi drivers their voice goes a bit more 'Walford', and if they're talking to the bank manager it might smarten itself up a little bit. So it depends on what company people keep, and it's trusting that the viewer or the listener is not going to go: 'that sounds terrible.' If you do it exactly as you hear it, there's some sort of magic takes place; people buy it and can be fascinated by it.

*What about the performance itself? Some actors who have worked with earpieces in performance, talk about it feeling like they are one step removed.*

I totally identify with that; because you are so busy listening to your fellow actors. Your instinct as an actor, if there is a laugh to be had, is to manipulate a line in order to boost that laugh, and it's stopping yourself from doing those things. It is about leaving your ego at the door; because as soon as you start manipulating the pauses, or the gaps, or the intonation, you're no longer doing your job. The reward comes from doing your job properly, rather than getting a massive laugh or making people burst into tears. Those things may well happen, but it's not your job to influence that. It's your job to say it as they said it, as much as you possibly can. And when everyone's doing that, something magical happens.

*It sounds very simple just to 'say it as they said it', but you're right, it is in contrast to how one might normally approach text. Was this a real challenge for you?*

It was difficult. It was technically the most difficult thing I've ever done – musically, and with the verbatim and the sheer amount of homework that you had to do on the accuracy. It's a slow burn, the reward for that, *London Road* is probably the most successful thing I've ever been involved in. When I first heard the music I thought 'I don't know what this is about. I don't understand it!', but it wasn't until it was all put together that it all made sense.

*When you were rehearsing* London Road, *was it one-to-one rehearsals?*

We did have set times with Alecky, we'd sit there and do the lines over and over again and she'd go: 'there's a little click in his voice there', or 'there's a slight hesitation.' There was one line where my character was trying to talk about 'machinations' or 'ramifications' or something, but he used the word 'munchuns', so he got himself confused – it's trying to work out what he was actually trying to say and what he ended up saying. It can be a bit like cracking a puzzle sometimes! Or when someone thinks about saying something, they start saying it and they change their minds, which happens all the time. It's trying to work out what they initially were going to say and maybe, because it wasn't politically correct or for some other reason, they ended up saying something else.

*Rufus Norris directed that production, with Alecky focusing on the detail of the voice and recordings; was he focused on the staging of it all?*

Absolutely, and also he'd say to Alecky: 'look, I want to progress the story in this way, have you got anything for that?' and he'd send Alecky off to listen to the hours and hours of material to see if she could come up with something. In the same way that someone produces a documentary, they want to shape the story in a certain way. So Rufus was far more focused on the whole story, and he left Alecky to deal with the minutiae of the tics and the accents. It wasn't a question of getting an actor to read a line in a certain way – that was already there. That job was already done; he didn't have to go through that agonising process where the director wants you to say a line in a certain way, but doesn't want to give you a line-reading. So that was one job he didn't have to do.

○   ○   ○

### Hilary Maclean

*Hilary Maclean trained at the Royal Scottish Academy of Music and Drama (now the Royal Conservatoire of Scotland). She was in the original cast for two of the most well-known tribunal plays, which were produced by the Tricycle Theatre –* The Colour of Justice *and* Bloody Sunday: Scenes from the Saville Inquiry.

HM: I did *The Colour of Justice* at the Tricycle Theatre and then we also did that at the Victoria Palace Theatre. In that I played WPC Bethel. The other piece I did was *Bloody Sunday*, also at the Tricycle, and we then took it to Belfast, and to Derry. It also then went on to Dublin but I was too pregnant so I didn't do that bit! Both plays were directed by Nicolas Kent and both adapted by Richard Norton-Taylor.

*RB: So were they your first experiences of working with verbatim theatre?*

Yes, they were my first. I should have said also that, in *Bloody Sunday*, I was playing Cathy McGahey who was one of the lawyers. But yes, *The Colour of Justice* was my first experience of being in a verbatim piece, but also my first experience of it at all – before that I hadn't even seen one.

*As an actor, what are the differences between approaching this and approaching any other play?*

**116**

I suppose, yeah, the first thing you have is the *importance*. The importance of the 'event', of the inquiry, to the *real* people involved and also to the wider community. I felt it especially with *The Colour of Justice* because the [Tricycle] theatre's in Kilburn, with a very large black community, so you felt very close to home with it. But it's the *reality* of it, it hits you immediately that this is a real situation, it's happening now and it means a massive amount to a lot of people.

The other thing I remember most was about the overall lasting effect – the education it gave me about racism, about one's own racism whether it's there or not, and about the institutional racism that was being questioned and tackled within *The Colour of Justice*. So before even starting talking about anything else, that's what's stayed with me the whole time.

*Both of these plays were about significant news events, that hit the national headlines, and for each there was lots of information available to the public. But was there information available to you about your character that wasn't so public?*

To be honest actually, as I was playing a police officer, you only have what's out there; they don't talk. I don't remember having an awful lot of access to very much else. I was given access to everything that she [WPC Bethel] actually said in court; obviously it was condensed, but not by much. I don't think there was any access [to her]; I couldn't go and look her up. I found that quite hard because it wasn't something anyone wanted to talk about. So she did what she needed to do at the inquiry, but other than that, no.

*And you didn't meet her?*

No, I couldn't meet her, no. And she was one of the less visible witnesses. Obviously not everyone's evidence was put into the adaptation, but there was something very key about her evidence which meant she needed to be in there to keep the story flowing through. But no, I didn't meet her. I didn't really have very much

**117**

more to go on. But playing McGahey [in *Bloody Sunday*], I had full access to her. She took me to her offices and playing a character on the other side of the bench was a very different experience, actually.

*With* The Colour of Justice, *did you find having that limitation on what you could get access to, that there was a feeling some people did not want you to do this play?*

Oh yes. There was a definite feeling of: 'it'd be better to let this all happen and then it can go away, be finished with and be dealt with in the proper lines.' But the play was bringing it back into focus in a really big way, the very fact that it ran and ran (and ran), you know it just kept going for six months – it was only supposed to be a short run at the Tricycle, but it just kept coming back!

But from the side of Stephen Lawrence's family it was the opposite. They were so supportive, they came along. The feeling we got from the community... so often I couldn't leave before end of the show, I never did. You were allowed to, but you'd just wait and sometimes you'd go in and watch the rest of it and feel the audience. You got something out of the audience, something unbelievable, and it would be very interactive.

The interaction of the audience was because it was the real thing and some nights they'd be getting involved and shouting! And I haven't been to an inquiry to know, but I suspect it was like that, people shouting at the lawyers and at the witnesses. And that interaction wasn't out of bounds, it was a very different theatre experience in that way.

Not so much with *Bloody Sunday*, although there was a little bit of that when we went to Derry but, with *The Colour of Justice* especially, you were part of an incredible experience. I think if you're doing a verbatim play in a place that's got local issues which are very important, it can be an incredible interactive and inclusive experience. Golly, yeah, it gives me the shivers actually, thinking about it.

But going back to research, for Bethel it was just the stuff that came from the courtroom, that's all I had. I didn't have anything else. But that's what you have and therefore that's what you worked with. And in that situation there was not much more that can be done, other than looking at how police hold themselves in witness situations within a courtroom. From that, you then have the limitations of the script and every 'ah' and 'um' is in there and is key and important and vital. And that was quite hard, but that's how I found her – cos she was from South London, so doing a South London accent and finding the rhythms, which is not my native accent. It's a great challenge, because you're not only doing a different accent, but you learn her speech pattern, the soul and the rhythm of her speech from what you have written down. It's sort of Pinteresque in that way – you must obey those. You chuck an 'um' in and it's wrong, that little gap, that little pause will say something which is incorrect; it might give an intention which is incorrect.

*So even though you had a limited amount of material to work from, would it be fair to say that there is still so much detail that you had to find pay attention to?*

The person I had to find myself, but Nicolas [Kent] and/or Richard [Norton-Taylor] had seen her so they could give me some information about how she was, how she held herself. But she was incredibly straight and very contained. They said she showed nothing, which I guess was fairly across the board with police witnesses, they just had to tell information and that's it.

*Tell us about the opposite experience, on* Bloody Sunday, *where you had access to the person herself.*

McGahey was fascinating, she was great. She was really lovely, very open and very keen to be involved and help the process. I met up with her and she took me to her chambers and just showed me the massive, massive files of stuff that she had to go through constantly. We chatted a bit and had coffee, just to get the sense of *her*. She was a very passionate woman, very passionate, and again she saw the importance of these things that they'd been working on for years. It mattered – all the people mattered. I only had one scene, but everyone remained onstage the entire time as a lawyer providing the atmosphere.

*As an actor, is it harder having to make your own choices, because you have nothing else (like with WPC Bethel), or was it harder saying: 'I know this woman, so therefore I know what's right and wrong' (like with McGahey)?*

Is it harder? It's just different. I knew Cathy was watching sometimes, I knew when she was in, so you try to hold with her mannerisms. But ultimately you just have to get on with it – it's provided in the text. You've got the speech patterns – the 'ums' and the 'ahs' and all of that so that's already in there. So having met McGahey and got *her*, I suppose it was slightly easier in some ways, I guess. Meeting the people involved does give you a sense of the whole, I think, but you do have pressure on yourself to make sure it's true.

*And did you speak to her afterwards, did she ever comment after the show?*

(*Laughing.*) I don't remember, I probably wouldn't have asked! But she was always incredibly positive and just deeply flattered, I remember she was just flattered that she was in there. They all did, they all found it quite funny, quite odd. A lot of them came along, some of the higher-profile lawyers came along as well, like Michael Mansfield QC, he was also involved with *The Colour of Justice* and he was very supportive.

*Did you feel pressure, because of the importance of these issues? Was there ever a moment of thinking: 'there's a lot of responsibilitiy on our shoulders to get it right'?*

To tell the story right, yes I think so, we all felt it. The focus was intense it was really, incredibly focused, everyone was, everyone felt the pressure. Especially, as I remember timing-wise with *Bloody*

*Sunday*, it was all happening at that time we were on. It was incredibly current; they were still working out what the result of the inquiry was going to be – that's why they put it on then. But it wasn't a bad pressure, it wasn't necessarily a negative thing. It was a *responsibility* which we happily took onboard. Everybody did. That's why they are such fantastic experiences, because you can't help but get involved emotionally yourself.

*Tell us about rehearsals; were there any significant differences in the rehearsal process?*

Yes, cos it tended to be just you! (*Laughs.*) You'd have your slot and you might not be in for another three days, so you don't really get a sense of it until technical rehearsals start. It'd be Nick at one end with his lectern, you in your witness box, and, of course, whichever lawyer was talking to you and that's it. And you'd have a slot, an hour, hour and a half maybe, so you'd go through it a few times and then you might be back in two or three days' time.

It's a very isolating experience, you've got to keep it going for yourself and it's all pulled together later on. I remember through the whole process your heightened sensitivity to anything that snaps on the telly... whether it was just racism itself, or whether it was about that particular inquiry, anything. Even after the play was finished, every time now Stephen Lawrence's name comes up I'm immediately wired in.

*And was that something you encouraged or did you try to resist letting this heightened awareness influence your performance?*

No; I see what you're saying, but I pulled it all in, because I felt it was all useful – to have a sense of the whole thing. Because, certainly in Bethel's case, or anyone in the police force, you can never know what they're thinking. All you're getting in verbatim theatre is what you've got from the inquiry, and you can't really know what they think – they actually know the situation, they know there is racism in the police force, but you can't know what they're *actually* thinking, so it's quite useful to take all that extra stuff in. That may differ from actor to actor, but I found it useful.

In Derry we went to the streets where it all happened, they took us round. That was massive for us; it was quite haunting and has stayed with me. It was a relative who showed us round and he'd obviously come to terms with it all, it had been so long you couldn't see any emotion, whether he was feeling it, you wouldn't know. He described all the different points, all the things we had been studying. We had studied a lot of pictures – photographs of Bloody Sunday are every-where as it was so well documented, but we were being shown all the stuff in the photographs, and where these things had happened and that felt very emotional. So I would suggest, whatever you're doing, getting into the environment where it all happened, that massively feeds your research. For *The Colour of Justice*, it was recommended that we didn't go to Eltham where it happened, but there were lots of photographs, from different perspectives of the point where it had happened to Stephen.

*Was there anything in particular that Nicolas Kent did in rehearsals to help you through that 'isolating' rehearsal process?*

Yeah, he and Richard [Norton-Taylor] gave helpful hints about Bethel, having seen her. If I was doing too much, being too expressive, he would say so. And he would keep it all very focused, very clear. I've always just loved when a director gives you the freedom to try stuff but this is not something you can really do that with. You can't say: 'I'm just going to try it like this'; so the most helpful thing he was doing was keeping me on track, to keep within the reality of the situation. So yes, he'd pick up on the 'erms', but we'd talk through what the 'erm' might have been about, or was it just a natural stutter? Ultimately, as long as you were saying the lines as straight as possible, keeping us on track was the most helpful thing he could do.

*I like the phrase 'saying the lines as straight a possible'; one might argue that our acting tradition and training has been built on actors finding out what is* unsaid *or what is* beneath *the line. Whereas with verbatim, because you are so focused on the specific syllables, the rhythm of what is* actually *said – is there still room to find what's happening underneath the line? Are you still thinking about that in the same way – or does it not even enter your mind?*

Gosh, yes, it's hard isn't it, because you're usually 'creating' things, you're right, usually as an actor you're creating a whole cushion of stuff and life around a character. But to invent that in this situation might mislead your delivery. So it is an odd thing, you have to just say: 'this is what she said and so this must be what she believes, and therefore that's what I believe for the performance.' I believed what she was saying, but as I say what you can't know is what she *actually* felt. It's a very interesting question though. Whereas speaking with Cathy McGahey, I could find out, I could ask 'so what do you think?' and she could give the other side of the coin.

*You mentioned earlier about the plays in performance and the audience's interaction. Why do you think the audience felt more able to interact? Was it to do with who the audience were, or the style of play itself?*

There were definitely people who came who didn't normally go to the theatre, who knew what this was about and wanted to feel it and be part of it and see it for themselves. Definitely some people who had never been before, which was brilliant to see. One of the most exciting things for me is to see people getting their feet across that threshold of a theatre. And that's one of the most important things about theatre, the fact it can change someone's mind about something; it can make you think differently about something. But yes, it may also be the format, just not feeling very 'play'-like – no curtain calls and just not very much happening, there's no movement. The drama is in the performance of the words, not in the physicality of it.

*It's interesting that Kent's productions broke with typical theatre traditions, like not having a curtain call. Was that just accepted by the audience? What was their response?*

Sometimes they wouldn't clap, but generally they applauded the performances, but there was no worry, nobody thinking: 'oh why didn't they come back on?', everyone accepted that. But then people would want to come and talk to you, so the post-performance was just as important. I remember meeting Stephen Lawrence's family and friends, and then in Derry I met people who were affected by Bloody Sunday and just the importance of what you were doing for those people came out mostly after the performances – so many of them came along and wanted to talk to you and tell you.

o   o   o

## Peter Temple

*Peter Temple was in the cast of* Where Have I Been All My Life? *by Alecky Blythe, a verbatim play set in Stoke and performed at the New Vic Theatre in 2012.*

*RB: You worked on a verbatim play that used Alecky Blythe's 'recorded delivery' technique through rehearsals and performance, can you talk a little about your experience working in the process?*

PT: The play was called *Where Have I Been All My Life?*, and it was put together by Alecky Blythe. And as I understand it, she went round the Stoke area – it was a local story to Stoke – and she just starts by saying: 'hello, can I come and talk to you?', with her tape recorder, and I don't think she knows really what she's going to be writing about until the people start speaking and she gets an idea of what's going on in their lives.

She spoke to several groups of people and realised that some of them were entering a talent contest in Stoke, which I believe was called

*Stoke's Got Talent*. But, of course, all with varying degrees of ability and very interesting people with very different lives, and the binding factor being that they all lived in the Stoke area. As far as I can work out, she followed these people in their run-up to performing in this talent contest, and she cut together the recordings into scenes. So she spoke to a group of women who worked in the factory, they were sitting in a pub with their husbands, and the first scene was that.

As actors you were allocated a character and she would play you the recordings that she had taken, into your ears on the rehearsal-room floor, through earphones. And you would listen to it, you would listen to what they say, so say somebody says [*in a Stoke accent*]: 'I'm going up that theatre, to register for that talent show, like.' Now you hear that voice in your ear and you, the actor, maybe listen to that a couple of times and then you're asked to repeat it exactly, with the stutters and the breath and whatever what you hear in your ears. You would start maybe half a second after you hear the first utterance. So if he says: 'I'm going up that theatre to see about entering that talent contest.' You'd hear: 'I'm going...' and you'd start with 'I'm going...', you see what I mean? You would talk along to the track, and, of course, through rehearsal you'd get to know what you're saying, but you mustn't pre-empt what you're saying.

We performed this play with earphones in our ears, so we were connected to the track of the play. That's how it works, and because you're listening to the voice in your head, it's in your ears, and talking over it, you can't hear the other actor opposite you talking – you can only hear her lines on the track. So it was a very strange thing; it was like being in your own world really, you're talking to another actor onstage, you can see her mouth moving and you can hear what she's saying but you don't hear *her* saying it, you hear the track saying it.

It was a fascinating rehearsal process certainly, but it makes for fascinating viewing as well because it soon becomes very clear to an audience that we are repeating things that we're hearing in our heads, and the one thing I always say about verbatim theatre is that you can't argue with it. For example, it went down extremely well in Stoke, but we had a Q&A one night after the show and one woman said: 'I thought it was disgraceful, I thought it was insulting, it took the piss out of the people of Stoke, it made them look stupid. Obviously somebody wrote it and hasn't got a clue about how people talk in Stoke.' And everybody in the room laughed, and we then told her: 'no, we're just repeating what is being said in our ears, those people exist and those people said those things.'

What that tells you is: you can't argue with verbatim theatre, because it has been *said*. You can't say: 'oh, people don't talk like that', because people *do* talk like that, and we can play you the recording. That was fascinating and it gives you immense confidence actually as an actor in performance. It makes everything alive and real – an actor isn't asked to interpret a text. A director and actor can't bugger up the portrayal of somebody's writing because you are literally just repeating what you hear.

Now you might make a character decision about how somebody *looks*, which is wrong. The subject of the play, the real people came to the press night and of course we had decided that we hadn't wanted to see photographs of these people (because we wanted to imagine them) and what was strange was when you met these people, how similar or how different they were to how you'd imagined them.

*And did they respond well to it when they saw it?*

They loved it, they loved it. I mean, some of them were shown in a pretty poor light and they'd say: 'I can't believe I really said that! Did I really say that? Oh my gosh!' They were all asked if they wanted to come and see the play and I think maybe twenty per cent of them said 'no', so the people who were there had a positive interest in it anyway, to be fair.

The skill in putting together the play was knowing what to put in and knowing what to leave out, where to put certain scenes, how it would all flow. I seem to remember a lot of the actors were positioned in the audience. The nature of what they were saying was generally conversational, and because it was generally in living rooms or shops, it

THE ACTORS

would have that feel about it, so if I'm sitting next to somebody in the audience and I suddenly turn to her and I say: 'well, of course, I started, I started, singing in the... er... the early sixties, y'know.' You say that to the person next to you and suddenly there's a light on you and everybody looks round – it was done in-the-round so everyone could see audience members all the time. It's a liberating way to work, actually, I would say, because you have the confidence that everything you say is very real.

*And was this your first experience of 'recorded delivery'?*

Yes, yes, I'd never done anything like that before. I think I'd done verbatim pieces before at drama school, but that was always off a script, so there would be the 'ums' and the 'ers' and the 'beg ya pardons', but you'd have to guess as to how that was done or how somebody spoke, what their accent was like. Whereas you knew exactly what this person's accent is because it's in your ear.

The director Theresa Heskins said it was quite interesting doing the auditions because some people could do it instantly and some people couldn't do it at all – they'd have this voice in their head and they couldn't concentrate. I imagine it's about how your brain processes information and how quickly or whatever.

o   o   o

# The Script

The layout of your script can make a huge difference to your actors. When transcribing your interviews, you will have to be consistent with the way you format your text and punctuation. This will be especially important if the actors are working solely from written text – if they don't have the recorded interviews in order to gain a sense of timing and pause, etc., they are more dependent on you and the clarity and accuracy of your transcriptions.

## Beats and pauses

- (*Beat.*) – generally taken as an involuntary short break in the sentence. It's surprising how we tend to ignore these little glitches in everyday speech and therefore we may not notice them at first when listening to an interview.

- (*Pause.*) – a longer break, perhaps as the character searches for a word or the next thought. These tend to be the moments an audience will 'read in to' and make judgements about.

## Punctuation

The **ellipsis** (...) and the **dash** ( – ) are both very common in the transcription of verbatim texts, as they are often used to indicate an incomplete thought. Often they are accompanied by naturalistic utterances such as 'erm...' or ' – ah – '.

More often than not they indicate where the thought has been interrupted – either by another thought from the same speaker or indeed by a new speaker altogether.

Many practitioners use a **slash** ( / ), which is an extremely useful way of indicating the moment in the speech when another character starts. When you are interviewing more than one person, there will inevitably be some overlapping of speech. Sometimes text is also laid side by side to indicate simultaneous speech (see Chapter Four for some examples of this.)

## Type

You will also need a way of indicating stress. Actors will always use their instinct to place the stress in the line, but with verbatim material this is *not* up for interpretation. Therefore you will need to find a way of clearly marking key words stressed by the interviewee. Avoid using *italics*, as conventionally these are used in playtexts as stage directions, most practitioners will instead prefer to use **bold** or an underline.

## Spelling

When an interviewee has a strong **accent** or **dialect**, you can support your actors by spelling words phonetically, rather than 'correctly'. It gives the performer another clue as to the distinctive speech patterns or particular habits of their character. For example: Dropped letters (such as the 'h' in 'have' might be noted as "ave'), or the pronunciation of an 'f' instead of 'th' (such as 'somefing').

## Character notes

Most actors and directors will spend time in rehearsals discussing the character. In this situation you may have been the one who conducted the interview and therefore are the only person able to share that information with the actor. Offer up all the details you can, no matter how obvious or insignificant they may seem. At the front of a script you'll often find a few notes about each character – their age, ethnicity, profession and so on. I also find it useful to note where the interview took place. Where we are has an effect on how we talk: we are likely to speak differently in our own home than we are in a more public place, like at work.

Three key words you'll need to bear in mind when preparing your text:

- *Accuracy*   Your responsibility is to be faithful to the original speaker and support your actors to be able to do likewise.

- *Clarity*   Be clear with your cast about your formatting choices. It might be a good idea to include a key at the front of the script for guidance, or talk your actors through your thoughts and processes.

- *Consistency*   Throughout your script, from interview to interview, be consistent with your formatting.

### Activity: Practice Makes Perfect

○ Search for a short extract of spoken text – most online news sites will have video content alongside their text articles. Alternatively, use your recording device or mobile phone to record a friend talking about, for example, their holidays or their first kiss.

○ Transcribe the text. Start by just focusing on getting down all the words spoken.

○ With a different colour, go back over the transcription and add in all the idiosyncrasies – the beats, pauses, accents, 'errs' and so on.

○ Rewrite the transcript adding in all your detailed vocal directions.

○ Give this text to a colleague and see if they can follow your transcription.

○ Play back the original voice recording – was there anything you missed?

# In Rehearsal

The director's role is to support the actors' efforts to faithfully replicate the voices from your research. If you are working with young or inexperienced actors, you may want to use some of the following activities to develop their skills and technique for this type of theatre.

Warm-ups are an essential part of an actor's preparation for work, either in rehearsal or performance. Even with experienced actors, focus your warm-up time on exercises that really develop your actors' listening and observation skills.

### Activity: Simple Listening Game

○ In groups of about five or six, the players stand in a circle.

○ Each person removes one shoe and places it at the feet of the first player.

- The first player throws one shoe to someone across the circle (not to either person immediately next to them). That person then throws the shoe to someone else, and so on until the final player throws the shoe back to the first. The shoe should visit everyone in the circle once before starting back at the beginning.

- The shoe keeps being thrown, always following the same pattern.

- When the group is ready, the first player introduces a second shoe, which also follows the same route. Then introduce a third… and a fourth?

- When the group is comfortably throwing three or four shoes, the last player begins to speak on a chosen subject (it could be anything from 'favourite holiday' to 'a frightening experience'). Once they have finished, the player to their left speaks on the same subject, and so on round the circle.

- Once everyone has spoken, the first player can begin to drop the shoes as they come back to them one by one.

- Now ask each person to recall the story offered by the person to their right.

## Activity: Simple Observation Game

- In pairs, the players stand opposite each other.

- In silence, one is the mirror to the other and copies exactly their body and facial movements. They might want to try focusing on just the face first and then taking in the whole body.

- Can the mirror follow their partner so closely that an observer is unable to tell who is following and who is leading?

## An alternative...

○ One person walks around the space while the other observes them and their natural walk – the speed, any obvious tension, arm-swinging, etc.?

○ Their partner then follows closely behind, trying to simulate the first person's walk. After a while, the first person steps to the side of the room and observes the second continuing to walk 'as them'.

○ The second person should try exaggerating the movements to create an extreme caricature, then return to the accurate replica.

## Activity: Voice and Body

○ Find a suitable extract of video – it could be an interview from the news, or a statement made by someone to camera, or footage of an interview you have conducted. (Try to avoid extracts where the speaker's voice is instantly recognisable.)

○ First play the cast the audio only.

○ Play it again, and this time ask them to note down one word to describe each of these *vocal qualities*:
  • Accent
  • Pace
  • Rhythm
  • Pitch
  • Timbre

○ Facilitate a group discussion asking the following questions:
  • *What is the subject being discussed?*
  • *How would you describe the speaker?*
  • *Where was the speaker?*
  • *What is the speaker's attitude towards the subject?*

*HINT: I find talking about 'attitudes' rather than 'feelings' helps achieve a richer, more detailed and ultimately more useful response from the actor.*

- Play them the whole extract – visuals and audio together.
- Facilitate a second discussion, asking:
  - *Is that how they imagined/expected the speaker to look?*
  - *Do the visuals tell a different story about the speaker's feelings towards the subject matter?*
  - *What about their surroundings; were they as expected?*
- Play the video again and ask the cast to note down one word to describe each of these *physical qualities*:
  - Gesture
  - Body language
  - Facial expression
  - Eye contact

*HINT: So often we rely on body language to supplement what we communicate in words. It may not be possible to have video or visual references for your characters, and exercises like this help us become aware of instinctive but perhaps misleading judgements we may make.*

## Activity: Uncovering Intentions

In Chapter Two, we discussed the importance of understanding an interviewee's agenda – why they wanted to tell their story. We also detailed an activity that may be useful for your actors during rehearsals. Actors and directors often talk of the value of playing a clear intention as a way of reaching a truthful portrayal of a character. It seems an entirely appropriate exercise for us, therefore, when the presentation of 'truth' is what verbatim theatre seeks to do.

- Identify when the speaker's 'intention' changes. It may change line by line, or it may remain constant through the entire speech/interview.

## Activity: Hot-seating

A simple acting exercise which will be familiar to most – a character is placed in the 'hot-seat' and asked questions by the rest of the group. The exercise works with an imagined character (such as Nora in Ibsen's *A Doll's House*) because, as actors, we have to remove the character from familiar surroundings (i.e. the play's narrative and location) and place them within an unfamiliar interview situation. With verbatim theatre, as the majority of our characters already exist within the realm of 'an interview', I would establish a more formal approach to this by asking actors to imagine these characters in fictitious and contrasting interview scenarios:

○ A press conference

○ A speed-dating event

○ A police interview

○ A job interview

This gives you the opportunity to ask questions you weren't able to ask originally.

*NB. The outcomes of this activity can in no way be passed off as verbatim material and must not be used as such in your play. It is simply a tool for the actor to gain a fuller sense of the character – perhaps to get to grips with information that has been discovered about them, but did not make the edited script.*

## Activity: Silent Improvisation

Without the constraints of the text, this exercise will enable the actors to explore the specific physical characteristics of the person they are portraying.

○ *Start with what you know*   Place the character in the situation in which you met them. Your actors may need your guidance if they did not meet the person themselves. If you have video footage, review it and discuss the significant physical characteristics.

○ *Recreate/copy and repeat*   The actors simply copy what they see and repeat simple movements. What do they notice about posture, pace and tension?

○ *Relocate*   Place the character in a location different to their original. It might be in a public place – a supermarket, a café or park. Alternatively it could be a private space – their kitchen, bedroom or potting shed.

   *HINT: These are real people, so it's worth placing them in real places – places they may actually be found in. It is not useful to imagine them in an extreme or overly dramatic location; the aim here is to practically explore the range of natural movement and physical energy that your actors will have to inhabit on stage.*

## Activity: Exploring Rhetoric

We've spent a significant amount of time identifying the agenda that lies beneath the words. What is the speaker trying to achieve? For some speeches, this will be overt, while for others it may be a little more subtle or perhaps even subconscious. It's similar with rhetoric – the use of persuasive language and form may be so blatant it's hard to ignore (the polished speech of a politician, for example); on the other hand, the speaker may employ many of these tricks and tools without realising. It will be useful for your actors to be able to spot these techniques in order to both understand why they are being used, and also to be able to replicate them.

In the previous chapter, I introduced the three main modes of rhetoric:

○ *Ethos: The credible argument*   'I'm authorised to speak on this subject and I have good intentions making this argument.'

○ *Pathos: The emotional argument*   'I'm showing you how I feel and I want you to feel how I feel.' (NB. This is about much about laughter as it is about tears!)

○ *Logos: The logical argument*   'The reason I think this way is because it is the truth (as I see it).'

Taking a particular speech from your material, can you and/or your actors identify where the speaker shifts from one 'mode' to another?

The more obvious tools of rhetoric will be familiar to all of us, especially those who paid attention in English lessons at school, as they form the basis of most creative writing. Here are just a few of the most common:

○ *Metaphor:* referring to one thing by talking about another.

○ *Simile:* directly comparing one thing to something else.

○ *Alliteration:* repeated use of the same letters at the beginning of words.

○ *Assonance:* repeated use of the same internal vowel sounds.

○ *Hyperbole:* overblown or exaggerated phrases (not usually meant to be taken literally).

○ *Repetition:* needs no explanation, the more people hear it, the more they will believe it (or so we often think!).

○ *The rule of three:* a golden rule for writers; examples, adjectives, reasons and so on seem to work best in sets of three.

○ *Antithesis:* setting one thing in opposition to another.

As a director, you are responsible for the facilitation of the performances. That means you have to provide an environment in which the actors feel supported and inspired. By 'environment', I'm referring to the physical rehearsal space; the amount of light, temperature, facilities, etc., are not to be taken for granted. You can also ensure the wall space is used to display your research – photos, maps and pictures, as well as the character target boards created earlier. Alongside the physical environment, a positive cultural environment is crucial to a happy and creative rehearsal room.

Below are a few **directing principles** for the rehearsal room:

• *Be accurate and clear*   My two favourite words in rehearsals; I expect them from my actors and demand them of myself.

As you require your actors to approach the text with accuracy and clarity, so must you. Be accurate in your analysis of the text and be clear in the instructions to your cast.

- *Provide the tools*    Give your actors everything they need, or everything you can, when it comes to techniques and skills, but also full access to the research. Are they able to meet the interviewees or at least see/hear the footage of them?

- *Be consistent*    As you have been with your script, so must you be with your actors. Pick up on the details of the text – every 'er' and 'um', every beat and pause, but do so consistently. One way of guarding against your own agenda creeping to the fore is to make sure you give each and every voice the same thorough investigation, preparation and rehearsal of text.

- *Listen*    You represent the ears of the audience and so need to make sure that the actors are replicating the interviewees in tone, accent and delivery. As a facilitator, it is also your job to listen to your actors which will make it easier for you to...

- *Be open to ideas*    Someone will have to make decisions and choices, and with their 'outside eye' the director is most often best placed to do that. However, be open to ideas from the company, as an actor's instinct, whether it is about blocking or cuts to the text, can often be very useful to you. It also values them as collaborators in the process.

- *Welcome failure*    Rehearsing is all about getting it wrong and trying again. Often the mistakes will lead on to a new discovery or an alternative idea. You may also have to reconfigure your script – cuts, additions, repositioning scenes and speeches; led by you, the whole company needs to be prepared to find their way through this 'work-in-progress'.

And finally...

- *Build an ensemble*    Like creating any piece of theatre, it takes trust. The actors need to trust you, your process, your research and your ideas. Likewise, you need to trust them, that they will be respectful of the material and the voices they represent.

# 8. The Staging

*How to approach staging and design to best explore, recontextualise and physicalise the material*

In my discussion with actress Hilary Maclean, she spoke of working on the famous tribunal plays describing them as '*not feeling very "play"-like – no curtain calls and just not very much happening, there's no movement. The drama is in the performance of the words not in the physicality of it.*' There is a distinct danger with verbatim theatre that it can become quite boring visually. The idea of watching a series of people sitting answering questions certainly doesn't set our pulses racing! We aren't creating radio drama and therefore we must think as carefully about the visual aspects of your production as we have with the text.

## Set Design

It is the job of the designer to create the world onstage. With imagined plays, the designer has free rein to use their imagination to create that world – is the castle at Elsinore in *Hamlet*, for example, a realistic castle or one more abstract and suggestive? The same is true for the verbatim play – your designer must create a world that supports the clarity of the storytelling, either by placing 'characters' in a semblance of reality or by offering a more abstract platform.

### Event-based Plays

With plays based on or around a specific event, it may seem most logical to base the set around a single key location. The place where you conducted your interviews may also provide the inspiration for your stage design (for example, if you've collected interviews from members of the public in the street) – it might seem appropriate for you to replicate that scenario, and therefore offer the audience an insight into the circumstances of your research. A good example of this would be *The Colour of Justice*. All of the text for Richard Norton-Taylor's 'script' was edited versions of the tribunal transcripts; therefore the set design recreated the room in which the tribunal was heard.

### Theme-based Plays

Likewise, for theme-based plays, the locations where the interviews took place may prove to be the best place in which to locate your play. Alecky Blythe's play *The Girlfriend Experience* doesn't focus on one particular event, it's a play that reveals the working and personal life of a group of sex workers. Alecky spent time with them in the communal living space, interviewing them in their own surroundings. As such, her stage direction at the beginning of the script is deliberately specific (although she relocated the setting to a different town):

> *A basement flat in Bournemouth. The action of the play takes place in the sitting room and the hallway. The view of the hallway is partly obscured. There are two bedrooms off the hallway. The kitchen is off the sitting room. In the sitting room there is a sofa, two armchairs, a television, and a small side table with a phone and a notebook.*[15]

15. Alecky Blythe, *The Girlfriend Experience* (Nick Hern Books, 2008, reprinted 2010, 2012), p. 4.

She goes further to clarify in her notes that the '*play is to be staged as if the audience were sitting in the room with the women. To this end, much of the dialogue is to be delivered as direct address to the audience.*'[16]

## Multiple Locations

It is highly likely that, in your broad research, you have spoken to lots of different people in different locations, and therefore need to think carefully about how to make reference to those differences visually in a way that supports the storytelling, rather than hinders it.

*The Power of Yes* by David Hare was performed on a very bare, open stage. Actors entered, often observing other speakers before or after their own speech, and they would take turns to introduce each other to the audience – many of the characters were high-profile public figures and some were simply introduced as 'a journalist', for example. What this simple staging was able to achieve was remove any sense of location, for these interviews all talking about the 2008 financial crisis – 'where' the interviews took place was not important. The space offered a blank box with only a LED screen used as a visual reference to aid the in-depth explanations of the complicated financial details. There were no seats on the stage, therefore everything kept moving and the piece gained a fluidity where it could have so easily felt staid and motionless.

This was all until the very last scene, in which the character of the interviewer visits billionaire George Soros in his New York apartment. In rehearsals, David Hare spoke to the cast of the experience of interviewing Soros, with his butler serving food prepared by his personal chef. The impact of the experience was directly translated on to the stage, providing the audience with as close a representation of that moment as possible.

In her play *Cruising*, Alecky Blythe introduces the audience to a number of characters but, unlike *The Girlfriend Experience*, she

16. Alecky Blythe, *The Girlfriend Experience* (Nick Hern Books, 2008, reprinted 2010, 2012), p. 4.

encountered them in different locations – some public, some private, but all have a connection to the interviewee and an effect (however slight) on the resulting testimony. *Cruising* was first performed at the Bush Theatre, London, and the designer was Anna Bliss Scully, who offers some insight into her process and the challenges of working on a play like this.

# In Discussion

## *Anna Bliss Scully on Her Design Process*

*Anna Bliss Scully was the designer for* Cruising. *She trained at the Wimbledon School of Art and is a freelance set and costume designer. As well as numerous verbatim plays and other new writing, she has also designed classical plays, opera and musicals.*

*RB: How did you first come to work with Alecky Blythe and verbatim theatre?*

ABS: In about 2004, a friend took me to see a workshop production at the Actors Centre that she'd designed the lighting for. The play, *All the Right People Come Here*, was my first encounter with verbatim theatre and with Alecky herself. What struck me at the time was how much emotional detail and social nuance was conveyed in Alecky's unique 'recorded delivery' technique. The play was essentially a comedy about social class, seen through the lens of visitors to the Wimbledon Tennis Championships; but the detail about relationships and the underlying emotions that you could pick up in the exacting verbal delivery, made it a far richer and more complex story.

Then in 2005 I worked with director Matthew Dunster at the Young Vic Theatre on a series of Shakespeare workshops. When he rang me a few months later to ask me if I was interested in working on a new play of Alecky's, I jumped at the chance! Since designing that production, *Cruising*, I have also designed another of Alecky's plays, *Do We Look Like Refugees?!* (National Theatre Studio and tour, 2011), and I worked on the original production of *London Road* at the National Theatre. In 2011 I also worked with an entirely different style of verbatim theatre on Gillian Slovo's *The Riots* at the Tricycle Theatre.

*Are the particular design challenges you face when approaching a verbatim play different to approaching a 'fiction' play?*

I'd say that designing for verbatim theatre presents challenges but also opportunities. In all the verbatim plays that I've worked on, the team (writer, director, designers and actors) have treated the characters with great respect during the rehearsal process: the words are real, and were spoken by individuals who may or may not ever see the play, but who all gave their opinions openly and honestly. That means, in a way, you feel a duty of care over those individuals and the way you represent them.

The fact that the text (or in Alecky's case, the recordings) has been edited and shaped into a storyline can present large practical challenges that are less common in traditional scripted plays:

- All of the verbatim plays I've worked on have had many more characters than there are actors available.

- The stories often move between many physical locations quickly.

- The timeline may not be linear.

All of these things mean that the design process has often been about finding the most efficient ways to tell the most complete story for each character. I've found that verbatim theatre is not the place to be indulgent as a designer; it really isn't about you and any fancy idea you might have: it is *all* about the characters and the story *they* are telling.

*Aside from having access to Alecky's research, what additional design research did you have to do?*

With *Cruising*, I was lucky enough to become involved at a stage when Alecky was still editing her audio. Alecky, Matthew [Dunster] and I spent time sat around her dining-room table with three sets of earphones on, listening through the recordings of the people she'd interviewed, and arguing for lines to be cut or added to the rehearsal draft of the 'script'. The 'script', of course, wasn't an actual printed text, but a CD of the show edit. It was slightly different with *London Road*, because of the songs – that cast did have a printed text and music manuscript – but every other time that I've worked with Alecky, all they've been allowed was an audio file or CD.

This audio is a surprisingly rich source of design detail, often telling you where in the world, and in what circumstances, the interview was conducted. I'm keen to find out: what's happening in the background? Does it sound like they're indoors or outdoors? Does the character sound happy, or stressed, or cautious? Are they throwing a ball to their dog as they talk? Or walking down the street? Or listening to music? It is all in there.

In addition to that, Alecky often snaps photos of her interviewees, or their homes. Sometimes I have wanted to see those to help the design process; sometimes I haven't.

In the case of *Do We Look Like Refugees?!*, which was set in a refugee camp on the outskirts of Tbilisi, I wanted to see all Alecky's photos, and did a lot of my own background research on the conflict between Russia and Georgia, which the characters had recently experienced. Because we wanted to convey to the audience a sense of the loss involved, I also sourced a lot of (quite harrowing) photographs of the conflict from news agencies around the world.

*With a play like* Cruising, *the audience meets various characters in different, specific locations – how do you achieve this, and take the audience to each one?*

I decided fairly early on in the process of designing *Cruising* that we couldn't be too naturalistic about our locations: we had to represent multiple rooms, in multiple homes, offices, a church, public buildings, a park... and all of it had to fit in the Bush Theatre's tiny auditorium. I boiled it down to a few essential design rules for our storytelling:

1. That if movement through a space was important to what the character was saying at the time, I needed to let them achieve that movement.

2. That the furniture I used must be flexible (and universal) enough to work in all of the story's spaces.

3. That I had to be fast transitioning from one space to the next, as we didn't want to stop the flow of the audio track.

4. That every part of the auditorium that I *could* include in our world, I would, so that the audience felt as connected to the characters' world as possible.

Ultimately the space became 'Alecky'. When she interviews people, Alecky asks multiple questions, gently teasing out their stories, and then she edits her voice out of the audio track. I felt that the theatre space and the audience in it had to become that one questioner; we were all in it together, silently listening, observing and teasing out the characters.

In practice, this meant cladding the entire perimeter of the auditorium in blue serge fabric from floor to ceiling. I remember the reason I used the colour blue for the walls was because I chose a fabric that matched the upholstery on the Bush's existing audience seating. Which makes total sense, I guess, given the desire to make the audience feel at one with the space: I matched the audience's environment, rather than acknowledging the normal division between them and the stage.

For furniture, I used two tables on wheels and a few chairs that could fit quickly together into multiple configurations to shape the individual scenes. We used as much of the real architectural shape of the theatre space as possible; for example, I had a stylised timber structure in an existing archway that became both a church's stained-glass window and a garden gate. Beyond that, everything else was done with selected props and costumes.

*Verbatim theatre is all about* real *words and* real *people, but in a theatre we are in an 'unreal' space. With your set, how bound are you to recreate a 'real' place?*

Every designer would treat this differently, I suspect, but I feel that the only thing I'm obliged to treat as 'real' in a theatre is the story. This means that if it tells the story best to have a real-*looking* world on stage, then I'll try to create that. Equally, if having a hugely abstract environment on stage is a better way to convey the 'real' atmosphere of the play, I will create that. For me, verbatim theatre is no different in that regard – I still can't literally take the audience to a pensioner's front room in Leominster, or to a refugee camp in Tbilisi – but I can help them understand something crucial about the context in which the character spoke. For me, hearing those words tell the story in the most coherent way is always my guiding light, and I will remove anything from the set that doesn't feel necessary to that journey.

*What about the characters' costumes; how closely do you copy the real person in what they wore?*

Costumes tend to feel like they need to be treated somewhat differently to the set in verbatim theatre. Every day we all read other people's clothes as an expression of their taste, class, age, wealth and profession, so we can really use costume as shorthand to drop us into a new character and their life very quickly. This is particularly useful in verbatim theatre as actors may be doubling up as lots of roles, and/or switch back and forth between multiple characters frequently. Many verbatim productions use simplified costume items (over a base costume) that can signify instantly which character the actor has slipped into, and tell us something about their world.

In verbatim theatre, you also deal with the added complexity that the real person you represent may be well known to the audience. I dealt with this a lot during *The Riots* at the Tricycle Theatre, as it featured testimony from many well-known politicians and public faces. As the costume supervisor on that show, it was particularly crucial to distil

146

the look of these well-known faces into one or more items that felt familiar, but not too distracting: a wig of an exact haircut; a specific colour combination of suit, shirt and tie; a particular style of hat. It felt especially important not to mock the characters with these choices, as we wanted the audience to recognise them, but listen to what they said before judging them.

*If you are just replicating real people in real places, are you still able to have a 'creative' process?*

I would say: absolutely! It is a very different process from designing pure fiction, but it is still possible to find ways to be creative. For me, it is about representing *not* replicating people, and there are worlds of possibilities in that small difference. You cannot tell the entire story of any contributor's life fully, with every detail; the creativity comes in deciding which details matter most to the story you are telling on that day, in that space, with those actors, and to that audience.

## Site-specific

It may be that you want to go a step further in bringing your audience into the world of the play. In this case you may opt for a site-specific production. One of the best examples of site-specific verbatim work I have encountered was *Katrina* by Jonathan Holmes. It was performed in a warehouse on London's South Bank. Moving through the building, the audience weaved their way through rooms decked out as accurate representations of New Orleans at various stages during the hurricane disaster that devastated the city. In each new space we found ourselves in a different location, encountering a different story.

When directing ACH Smith's play *Walking the Chains*, deciding upon a venue was a challenge in itself. We had to take into consideration the subject – the Clifton Suspension Bridge – as well as the particular challenges of the text – the ensemble nature and the idea that the play shifted location and constantly moved back and forth between the modern day and the 1800s.

Also, we knew from the start that this production was to involve circus performers, and so we needed a venue that was large enough to hold the substantial amounts of rigging structure needed to support acrobats. The production's designer, James Helps, suggested we look at the Passenger Shed, which adjoins Bristol Temple Meads station. This was perfect, as it was certainly large enough, but it also had the direct connection with Clifton Bridge, through its architect, the Victorian engineer Isambard Kingdom Brunel. It's crucial with a found space that it serves both purposes – a functional space to house the performers and audiences as well as making a significant contribution to the atmosphere of the event.

Smith's script contained no stage directions at the beginning of each scene, which allowed my production not to be locked into any one location; it was, instead, constantly shifting and transforming the space from one place to another. I was clear I wanted the stage 'in traverse' between two banks of audience, making them, in effect, the Avon Gorge that needed to be bridged. This idea gave my production a clear context. A play about the bridge, set in an historically connected location, and investigating themes of bridges and crossings, informed how I physically used the space.

It was a production that relied upon an ensemble of actors, who were constantly shifting, moving and transforming, both as characters and scene-shifters. One moment they were modern-day visitors on a tour of the Clifton Bridge, and the next they were the eighteenth-century navvies building it. Like many verbatim plays, the cast played several parts each, so establishing a language with the audience whereby it is possible that the space can change in an instant, as could any actor, was key. The presence of the ensemble gave definition to the space from moment to moment.

My other asset was the troupe of circus performers who were part of the ensemble but would erupt from the crowd with bursts of energy and physicality. Isambard Kingdom Brunel's engineering feat is often referred to as 'audacious' and as writer, designer and director, we all agreed that circus would bring to life that sense of audacity while at the same time providing us with a tool with which we could physicalise the laws of physics and engineering.

## In Discussion

### *James Helps on Designing* Walking the Chains

*James Helps is a production designer for film, television and theatre. Amongst others, he has designed productions for the Tobacco Factory (Bristol), Nuffield Southampton Theatres, Theatr Clwyd and the Lyric, Belfast. In recent years he has designed several site-specific productions for Show of Strength Theatre Company, Bristol.*

*RB: Can you tell me a little about how your design process began on* Walking the Chains?

JH: Before we began, we had some development money to workshop an early draft of *Walking the Chains* at Circomedia, the Bristol circus school. We worked for a week with four actors and four circus performers. We began with a meet and greet, at which I remember you asked me to get a variety of tools, boxes, buckets, a small barrel, a straw bale, brooms and shovels and planks. Nothing was characterised or particularly related to the text but they were things to play with. At the same time Circomedia gave us circus rigging, ladders, ropes, etc.

The space itself was draped in fabric to hide damp walls, had ropes tied off to rigging points; there were hoops and trapezes and it brought to my mind how Bristol must have looked in its harbour in the years before the Suspension Bridge, before the GWR and Brunel's steamships. The actors improvised bridges and could climb and twist, slip down both ropes and silks, and were all at ease with their bodies within the space, able to make themselves into the script and to take the script and make it part of themselves. As Brunel says in the play: 'we had begun.'

An overall image for the show was discussed, and I showed the team a Banksy of a ballerina walking a slack rope the shape of our bridge's chains, except on the reverse of a painting and so representing the string that would have hung on the wall. It remained a significant image for me when designing the piece.

*It was a fun week, exploring the themes of the play, where the historical stories connected with the modern ones. But also an opportunity to ask more specific questions, like: 'how are we actually going to show Brunel stuck in a basket midway across the gorge?'*

I like to watch a director working with the actors, blocking sections of the play to see how the story can unfold within the space. You were clear from the outset that you wanted to play the bridge's story in traverse. We looked at other options, but even the aesthetics of the venue demanded a breadth of the bridge filling the space.

After planning on paper, I moved to modelling the space (having to reduce the scale to a quarter of the accepted scale or the model would have needed a stretched Transit van and a huge budget itself to complete!). The modelling stage began with looking at the seating plan. We were tied to creating a seating capacity of 500 for each performance. Each seating unit sat about sixty-five and the simple arithmetic required four units in a line each side of our acting area. This meant that we had a long playing area of over sixty feet from where the actors could enter and exit.

It was an obvious decision to split each of the sides down the middle, halving the possibility of maximum entrances for the audience relating to the cast. Though this also stretched our acting area, we were trying to give a sense of the astounding bridge itself – at the time of its construction, the longest suspension bridge in the world!

As the script developed, we needed to include spaces for community choir and a band, to create a bar as well as an exhibition area, and to create a safe and secure ticketed entrance. This was becoming an event, from audience arrival until their departure, and it had to be created within the empty space of the Passenger Shed.

*Yes, the challenge was that your design had to encompass the whole space, not just the acting area.*

I have for many years played with the idea of containing not only the actors and the action within the space, but of including the audience within the same conventions. Our actors could appear from either or both ends, but now also enter from the centre. I added a raised walkway seven feet above the ground and behind the audience. I imagined this as being an area from which our choir could sing.

Next came the idea of a second raised thrust on each side above our centre entrances. This would allow us to create the first images of building a bridge to the centre of the playing area and we wondered how we could span the gorge.

*So once we had set on the audience configuration and you had a vision for shape of the space, how did you then start to think about the specifics of the play?*

The initial workshops and then watching rehearsals unfold were my main references; rather than 'design' the show, I started a storyboard using the script to suggest how we could move the performance with a fluidity that allowed one scene to cross-fade as a new scene began elsewhere. Whatever your point of view, we were able to engage the audience across the width of the gorge.

The story was never linear. The play didn't tell the story in the order that it happened, but moved from past to present. It reflected both ACH's historical research as well as the contemporary interviews he had collected, so the space had to be flexible enough to allow us to move between the historical and modern. I was really keen that the show included circus from the outset and suggested a barrel being walked down our street/gorge/river at the beginning of the show. This floor was stencilled with blue cobbles and also included the seating-block numbers in the way that the docks were marked up with information.

Behind the audience were the coloured hills that surround Bristol and beyond. The hills were white cloths hung from our rig to contain us all (performers and audience) within the world we created within our gorge. At each end was a raised level. At the far end was a bricked, raised area for our lighting board and stage manager, and at the other end was a similar bricked wall with a larger but lower platform, just a step up from the playing area that contained the band, a keyboard and drum kit, with our composer and trombonist. Each end of the truss had ropes and pulleys that allowed silks to be pulled up from the floor giving the shape of the towers at both sides of the bridge. As well as the ropes, there were also long rope lights that, when joined for the finale, were illuminated to create the sweeping, night-time view of the bridge that we Bristolians take for granted, yet still fires the soul.

*We had a large company too, and we were both keen they were a unified group who changed the space and characters quickly, but the audience couldn't differentiate between musician, actor or circus performer; was that a tough challenge?*

We spent a long time working out who that group was and settled on making them a group of navvies (the Victorian workman who built the bridge). The show began with a big tease, music and song, the bustle of a pre-bridge Bristol, labourers and the varied people of Bristol jumbled up together. It was expressive of the ensemble nature of the piece, no one was particularly a circus performer or an actor, everyone, including the choir, had a character and a performance to give.

Everyone had a generic workman's costume – timeless, but with a hat or a skirt and a jacket that would appropriately allow characters to change within a scene, onstage in full view of the audience. The craft of our players was extraordinary, facilitated by careful rehearsal and the sense of security that comes from a single shared vision. Ropes would lift an assortment of bales, then barrels, and even actors on ladders way up into the air, delighting the audience but always driving the story.

## Activity: Physicalising the Text

*HINT: For this activity you can use any of the text extracts in this handbook. Alternatively you may want to use some of your own material and use this exercise to explore staging your script.*

○ *Units of action*  First, break the text down into units of action. A unit ends when the energy or dynamic of the scene changes – in a fiction play this may be the entrance of a new character, or the revelation of the new information. If you are working with a large cast you might choose to break off into pairs or small groups and take one unit each.

○ *Highlight the clues*  Search for the clues in the text that relate to movement and location – literal and abstract or thematic. (e.g. in *Walking the Chains* there were several literal references to different modes of transport and flight, but also the constant references or inferences to the 'bridge', and crossing the bridge, were prominent and suggestive of movement).

*HINT: Small sections of the text are easier to manage, rather than attempting to approach the whole scene.*

○ *Stillness*  Read through the unit while sitting down. Try to recreate the speaker telling a story to the interviewer. Now try it standing up. Try altering the configuration of all the characters – some seated, some standing, in a circle so everyone can see everyone else, then perhaps move some people out of the sight of others. Wherever they are positioned they must keep still, but continue to vocally express their story and all the information in it. What effect did each different configuration have on the voices? Which configuration best supported the words of the text?

○ *Movement*  Begin to add small amounts of movement – perhaps some characters can move while others can't. Perhaps each character is allowed one natural gesture. Allow the characters to move freely. Try asking them to carry out simple tasks while speaking – painting a fence, drawing a picture, chopping vegetables, for instance. What do you gain from movement? Or what do you lose?

○ *Choral movement*   Take a short speech (or section of a speech) from one character. While one actor reads the text and remains still, give the others simple tasks or movement instructions around them. Return to the clues you highlighted in the text – how can the ensemble embody or physicalise them? Is it 'real' activity or abstract movement? Does it help support the giving of information, or help create a significant atmosphere or environment?

### Activity: Creating the World

*HINT: As a director, you will have to give your designer a brief – a clear understanding of the story you want to tell and the 'world' you wish to create on stage.*

○ *Describe the world*   On scraps of paper, write down all the adjectives that you would use to describe the world in which these characters exist. If you are using your own text, you may wish to refer back to your interview notes.

○ *List the locations*   Write down all the key locations, either referenced by the characters or inhabited by them.

○ *Combine them together*   Place all the adjectives you noted earlier around the location it best describes. Are there some descriptions that don't match, but stand out in contrast?

○ *Create that world*   Use whatever you have to hand and turn your space – rehearsal room, classroom or whatever – into that world. Can you find ways to encompass every aspect? How might you carry this forward to become a set?

*HINT: By starting with the resources immediately available to you and your cast, you eliminate the need for vast expense. Think carefully about the world and locations you are required to create, and then work out what is essential to enable you to create that?*

As director, you will be seeking to create an onstage world in which your verbatim piece can live and thrive. As always, all your decisions need to be checked against our recurring question: 'does this support or enhance the storytelling or does it distract from it?' If the answer is the latter, you'll need to reassess and adapt the ideas accordingly.

> *HINT: Be specific about what works and what doesn't. If your staging or design ideas aren't working, you may not have to throw the whole lot out and start again. Think carefully about what precisely isn't working about it. A small change can make a huge difference!*

## Using the Ensemble

Your greatest asset is your company, so in thinking about how to employ them to the best advantage, you may wish to consider the following:

- *Doubling*   As Anna Bliss Scully described, you may need to have actors switching between different 'characters'. Think about how you double up your actors between the parts they are playing – if they appear too close together, will the audience get confused? How will they be costumed to assist clarification? Are they similar in physicality and 'voice', and so hard to differentiate?

- *Creating atmosphere*   Are the ensemble on stage throughout? If so, what are they doing – observing, like a Greek chorus, or detached in their own worlds? Is there pre-show action – do the audience enter a world already busy with activity that sets up the tone and atmosphere from the very top of the show?

- *Encompassing the audience*   In the production of *Where Have I Been All My Life?*, Peter Temple described the company being amongst the audience; equally, Anna Bliss Scully mentioned matching the colour on stage to that in the auditorium. How can you use the ensemble and/or your stagecraft to draw your audience into the story and make them feel part of the action?

# 9. ■ The Golden Rules

By way of summarising lots of the information in this handbook, I asked the practitioners for their top tips for creating verbatim theatre. Here's what they said:

## Interviewing

### *Alecky Blythe*

- The feedback I often get from actors in my workshops is: 'I don't know how to interview all these people, I feel so nervous.' I say, you have to think of it like an actor – I came to verbatim work as an actor in the first place. When you are interviewing you have to connect with the actor side of you, almost like playing the part of an interviewer. I can hear it in my voice when I listen back to my interviews – it will give you a confidence. You'd be amazed how many people say: 'oh, I haven't got anything to say,' and half an hour later you're still talking to them!

- You have to find people you connect with. Trust your instincts – if you have a connection with an interviewee, if they make you laugh or move you to tears, then chances are they will do the same to the audience. The audience are human too.

- It takes a long time! There aren't really any short cuts – I came into verbatim work when I had time on my hands as an out-of-work actor. You'll record hours and hours of interviews, but you have to sift the wheat from the chaff. But when you find that story, when you find that gold dust, the hard work is worth it.

### ACH Smith

- Before you start, do what you can to set up a friendly feeling with the interviewee.

- Be honest about what you're up to.

- Attend closely to what they say to you.

- Allow the conversation to digress if it wants to. It is likely to lead to things you hadn't thought of, but will be glad to have gathered.

- Before you leave home, always check your Dictaphone is working and ready. (I once conducted a long interview with Joan Plowright, who had a dragon-like reputation, but was in a good mood. On the train back I found that my tape was blank. I had been lazy enough not to take notes. In a muck sweat I had to strive to recall what she had said, phrases she had used. She never sent me a reproach, which may be a tribute to my memory, but was more likely boredom with the blandness of what I'd written.) So, if you use a Dictaphone, also make notes. Better, if you can get an assistant, let them make the notes – so you are not distracted.

# Writing/Editing

### Patrick Sandford

- I would say immediately, you have to *want* to tell the truth. Verbatim theatre is about telling the truth, and your piece of theatre will be as good as the importance to you of the truth you are telling. If you feel passionately about the truth of the story you are telling, that passion will come across to the audience – but you cannot inflate or invent that passion.

- Verbatim theatre has to start with the words of the people, and they may not say the things you want them to say – they may not give you the dramatic headlines that you want.

- It's quite hard to show off in verbatim theatre; if you do start showing off, then I think there might be a problem. If you want to make a really good *showy* piece of theatre, then do *Bugsy Malone*! Verbatim, of all forms of theatre, is in a way the most generous because you're using your skills entirely at the service of the people whose conversations you're listening to. It's a very generous art form in that sense and a very beautiful art form. Of course, it needs to be theatrically interesting, but it's tempting to want to develop and expand the theatrical imagery at the expense of the truth.

- It's not your job to educate with a capital E – remember you're not telling the *whole* truth, it's not a doctoral thesis that covers every aspect, but personal accounts. Verbatim theatre shouldn't be preachy – any message should just emerge from it.

## Acting

### *Hilary Maclean*

- You need to have an open mind. Whatever you believe, whatever you feel, you still have to remain open as an actor. That's the main thing. Get to know the person you're playing as best you can, and don't make judgements; I think that's quite hard, not to judge.

- If you can go and connect with the environment where the events depicted in the play took place, do. If not, get as many photographs as you can, especially if it's a local issue.

- Talk about it. Talk about the whole thing, talk about it with other people, so you learn from it. Society always has something to learn from these events and I think you as a person can also learn from it. It's amazing, so many things you think you know about and then all this stuff is unearthed and you realise you know nothing about it at all!

### Peter Temple

- I would say to practise with your friends – put a tape recorder in the room when you're next with your friends and then, when they've all gone, listen to that tape and see if you can imitate the voices that you hear.

- From the point of view of putting together a piece, one of Alecky's fantastic skills, and the reason her work is so successful, is because of her personality she's able to put people very much at their ease, so that they feel they can be themselves. So what she manages to do, and I don't know how, is make them forget that they are being recorded. I think if you're going to do this, you need to get your subjects to be totally at ease so you get to see them 'warts and all', so that they are not putting on a façade and everything that you hear is terribly, terribly real.

### Paul Thornley

- Put the hours into the *specifics* of it.
- Leave your ego at the door.
- And get out of your own way as much as possible.

## Designing

### Anna Bliss Scully

- Respect the story: what is the story that you and your collaborators are trying to tell? Find a way to tell that, and tell it well. Ignore the rest.

- Respect the characters: even if you disagree with their opinions, or want your audience to laugh at a character, you must respect them all. Let the audience meet them for the first time (just like you did) and make up their own minds.

- Find out everything you can: do your research, whether that means background news stories, pictures of real people and what they wear, pieces of music... Most of it won't make it into the show, but all of it will inform what you choose to show on stage.

- Take it all out and put it back in: this applies to all plays, but is especially relevant to verbatim. If you have a model box (or a drawing, or idea) that isn't working, take everything away and argue with yourself for every single item to go back in. Some stuff won't make it back in, and that is the best thing that ever happened to your design: what remains is the pure concentrate.

- Leave your ego at the door: verbatim plays tell somebody else's story; the best design to tell that story might be more functional or 'ugly' than you'd like, but go with it. Be lean, not indulgent; rise to the challenges, don't moan about them. You will find a way to solve the practical problems elegantly if you remember that it's not about you.

## And finally...

...from me, my top-five tips for the director, creator, facilitator – all of these in fact – indeed, for the **Verbatim Theatre Practitioner**.

- **Be accurate** – with your notes, transcripts and rehearsal scripts.

- **Be clear** – with your interviewees, your collaborators and your actors.

- **Be bold** – with your decisions and creative with your staging.

- **Be careful** – as in 'full of care'. You are the custodian of this testimony; look after it and treat it with respect.

- **Be truthful** – to yourself in your decision-making, to your interviewee and company about your intentions, and most importantly to your audience in the telling of your story.

# Acknowledgements

First and foremost, I would like to thank Matt Applewhite and John O'Donovan at Nick Hern Books – Matt, for having the confidence in me and the patience to get the book going, and John, as my editor, for brilliantly guiding me through the process.

Thanks also to the following for their contribution or their support in the creation of this book:

Michael and Karen Belfield, Sandra Theresa Buch, Anna Bliss Scully, Alecky Blythe, Ivan Cutting, Jonathan Goodwin, Linda and Peter Grundy, James Helps, Neil Kendall, Hilary Maclean, Roger Lawrence, Tim and Helen Robinson, Patrick Sandford, ACH Smith, Peter Temple and Paul Thornley.

o   o   o

The author gratefully acknowledges permission to quote from *The Girlfriend Experience* by Alecky Blythe and *London Road* by Alecky Blythe and Adam Cork (both published and reproduced by permission of Nick Hern Books); and *Walking the Chains* by ACH Smith (reproduced by permission of ACH Smith).

**www.nickhernbooks.co.uk**

facebook.com/nickhernbooks

twitter.com/nickhernbooks